Osprey Colour Series

MAMMOTH TRUCKS

MODERN DAY HEAVY, HEAVY HAULAGE

BOB TUCK

Published in 1985 by Osprey Publishing Limited
12–14 Long Acre, London WC2E 9LP
Member company of the George Philip Group

British Library Cataloguing in Publication Data

Tuck, Bob
  Mammoth trucks: modern day heavy, heavy haulage.
  —(Osprey colour series)
  1. Trucks
  I. Title
  629.2'24   TL230
ISBN 0-85045-616-9

Editor Tim Parker
Printed in Hong Kong

Front cover TRL 924H (on the right) may be getting
rather long in the tooth now but as a winch tractor
Econfreight think much of her so that on occasion she is
taken to site piggy-backed on a low loader so that she
can show off prowess and be utilized. She is seen in the
premises of RGC at Methil in August 1983 assisting
MGE 180V in the site movement of one of two
integrated deck sections for the Rough storage project.
This mountain of a load weighed in at over 1720 tonnes,
although even this wasn't evenly distributed throughout
its mass. Meticulous attention had to be paid to the
design of the steelwork that was placed underneath the
load to spread the weight evenly through the modular
trailers

Back cover Whessoe Heavy Engineering of Darlington
installed 4600 tonnes of large pipes underground at the
Dinorwic pumped storage station near Llanberis, North
Wales. To transport these pipes, which were up to 15 ft
in diameter and 130 tonnes in weight, Whessoe bought
XDC 485S, an 8 ft 2½ in. wide Scammell Contractor and
ten rows of dished Cometto axles which could act as two
five-row bogies. The Scammell had 31.5 tonnes of ballast
on its back as it was expected to inch its 200 tonnes of
weight up wet gradients of 1 in 8. On completion of the
job the Scammell was sold to Wrekin Roadways whilst
Sunters were to buy the trailer

Page 1 Anyone hauling excessively large abnormal loads
out of Immingham docks are well aware of the height
limitations imposed by the NCB conveyor bridge. In
winning the job to move the two coke drums from
Thornaby, Econofreight Heavy Transport had first to
convince their clients that they could squeeze under this
obstruction without touching it. Checking the clearance is
mountaineer Eric Pinchen whilst project manager Toby
Allin, sporting hard hat, prefers to keep his feet on the
ground. The trailer used was a four-bed six Nicolas,
three-file wide, with 120 tyres

Contents

Title page With a capacity of 64 tonnes plus an ability to get in and out of places where virtually no other semi-trailer could go, Hallett Silbermann thought very highly of this rear steer Craven Tasker low loader seen posed for the photograph near Colnbrooke in 1978. However, with changes in the way highway engineers look at these things, this load carrier built by Taskers with four axles, two sets of two in-line, was reclassified as having only two axles each with eight tyres in-line and it was thus superseded by the multi-axle, hydraulically suspended trailer. John Macklin is at the wheel of Volvo F89 (SMJ 292R) which was rated for 100 tonnes gross operation whilst its load is an RB base crawler machine used by Wests Piling and Construction which Taskers reckoned could be loaded within seven minutes of the unladen outfit arriving

LONG VEHICLE

PHY
21M

LONG VEHICLE

LONG VEHICLE

Introduction

I've always been passionately interested in trucks, although it wasn't long ago we all called them lorries. This is my third book but the first of nothing but colour photographs. It's a fascinating business especially that of the real specialists in very heavy haulage. I have tried to select a wide spectrum of such haulage in the United Kingdom, the majority of which have not been seen before.

I would like to thank all those people who have assisted in research or with the furnishing of photographs. Those specifically I would like to mention are David Alderson, John Banks, David Collins, George Curtis, Jack Hill, Tom Llewellyn, Chris Miller, Andy Munroe, Robert Price, Brian Rodwell, David Silbermann, Brian Stenning, Peter Sunter, Tim Wayne, Jon Whowell, Henry Wood.

Bob Tuck
Yarm, Cleveland
January 1985

Left The modern day trend in construction finds lots of objects manufactured in total at the factory so that upon delivery the load is simply lifted off its transporter and placed in position virtually ready to go to work. The specialist heavy haulier who has to bridge the gap between start and finish accepts the problems of difficult transportation. Chris Miller hauled four of these awkward columns out of Adamson and Hatchett at Dukinfield during 1981, destined for BP at Grangemouth. Stuart Bell is at the wheel of PHY 21M, the faithful 6×4 Volvo as he reverses out of the manufacturer's premises. Tony O'Pray is steering the two-line Cometto bogie which was specially modified by Miller to make it useful for this sort of work

7

1
Larger than life

Left Like any heavy haulier worth their salt, Pickfords pride themselves on being able to produce a suitable outfit no matter what the job. But have you ever seen an MAN - 4 axle extendable King artic carrying such a heavy load that it had to be supported on a Crane solid tyred trailer and then be headed-up by a 240 tonne GTW Scammell? Fife-based William Hill's photograph appears to portray just that. There are, in fact, two seperate loads both built by Largo Lintec of Methil which have been squeezed on to the *Saint Brandan* and pictured in Methil harbour in 1978. Bound for St Fergus, a 23 ft running height discounted the normal direct haul, the two loads going by water as far as Fraserburgh and thence by road to site

Below Conditions may not have been ideal for photographer Robert Price but Wynns' last mighty Pacific *Dreadnought* is always worthy of inclusion. NDW 345G is the second version of this tractor which originally bore the registration of GDW 277, its immense modifications including more than a fair share of Scammell bits under the Pacific skin. She is seen on 30 November 1975 at Tilbury Docks where the 160 tonnes of Brush alternator that was hauled from Loughborough is being transferred from the ten-line Nicolas trailer to the *Neuenburg* prior to passage to Kuwait

Left With Jimmy Goulding watching Ken Ward doing the drawbar leap, LAJ 798P pushes this Whessoe pipe from Number Four quay at Middlesbrough Docks onto the *Kingsnorth Fisher* prior to passage to North Wales. Sunters were involved in 22 of these shipments destined for CEGB's Dinorwic power station and on each occasion the ships were loaded to their full capacity. The penstock vessel already on deck was one of the last constructions made at the old Ashmore factory in Stockton prior to closure. To ensure it got as far inboard as possible the hydraulics on the leading bogie were lowered whilst the trailing bogie raised its suspension to crank the load inwards. Kingsnorth was the second of these two Fisher boats although it and the large dock cranes are virtually dwarfed by RB's floating crane *Telford* seen in the background

Below During June and July 1979, whilst the relevant part of ICI Wilton was on shut down, Sunters moved three skid-mounted modules inside the works. The first unit was moved by ballasted Volvo HVN 396N using two Crane bogies whilst the second was pulled the short distance by the well turned out Titan VVN 910S in articulated form. The tractor is seen to have a massive wheelbase and although bought to pull a semi-trailer is regularly converted to ballast box form. She is coupled to a King semi-trailer with hydraulic neck, steerable back bogie, 30 ft well and 60 tonne capacity, their combination able to haul its charge to the unload point with little difficulty. The third module, seen in the background, had a more chequered journey

Above Magnaload is a grand sounding title for a heavy haulage company. Unfortunately the name was only actively used through the second half of the 1970s. RAJ 530R was the second of two F89s bought by the company; both were rated for 180 tonnes gross train weight for 7.5 per cent gradeability. It was, however, operating in excess of 200 tonnes GTW when observed leaving Carlisle in the early hours of 12 December 1979 with Lenny Peacock at the wheel. The 130 tonne railway crane built by Cowans Sheldon and destined for New Zealand was one of two hauled in convoy down to Workington docks, being carried on 12 rows of Scheuerle running gear

Left NAJ 103P, Sunters' *Fearnought* provided the pulling power for this third module with driver Peter Clemmett applying his feet to both its pedals. Hauling the load into the confines of ICI, the Scammell was obliged to stop as it came down the road front right of shot on approaching this rather substantial pipe bridge. To negotiate the obstruction a JD White Demag TC 1200 mobile crane picked up the load and it is seen in the top right of photograph waiting for the Sunter crew to bend the trailer round the corner. Even with all-wheel steering, the Nicolas load carrier needed all of the roadway and a little bit more. Being two trailers side by side, its configuration is termed as four-file wide with the join up the centre clearly on show. Guiding its direction is steersman Gordon Shepherd who has his hands on the controls at the rear nearside

Right During the early 1960s Wynns' engineers constructed a lifting gantry primarily to place steel converters into position in the Llanwern steelworks. Twenty years on, the same gantry has been adapted and used for a multitude of other purposes one of which is shown in this George Crawford photograph as it assists in the loading of a 25.6 tonne 55 ft long drilling head at Prestwick Airport. With the price tag of a new Boeing 747F cargo plane quoted around 100 million dollars, it is not the sort of thing which permits mobile cranes to load independently into it. This particular load was lifted on to the gantry allowing the plane, with nose lifted open, to be pushed as far forwards as possible absorbing the column as it went. The smooth control of the co-ordinated power jacks then lowered its load on to the roller-decked cargo floor and assisted as winches pulled the drilling head right inside

Below TSL, Transport Services (Lindsey) Ltd. is a wholly owned subsidiary of the massive Consolidated Land Services Group based at Scunthorpe. The seperate identity is maintained as TSL's small fleet specializes solely in heavy haulage. They have also maintained seperate vehicle contracts for CLS are mainly Mercedes-Benz, TSL are nearly all Volvo. The F12 6×4 tractor fitted with torque converter rated for 240 tonne GTW operation is highly favoured and John Thompson is pictured at the wheel of XTC 638V which can either be used in articulated form or as a ballasted unit. John is seen on a local move in Scunthorpe during 1981 when TSL were moving boilers from Normanby Park to Appleby Frodingham steelworks. Resting on a King tri-axle semi-trailer, this near 60 tonne lump had a running height close to 22 ft on its five mile journey

Chris Miller has done lots more heavy haulage work than their time at Dinorwic but these Mike Jarvis photographs taken inside the Elidir mountain are certainly typical. This near 30 tonne Thyssen winch drum was one of several moved out of the mountain after they had been used in the initial construction of the main shafts. Although Peter Beasley doesn't appear to have much space in which to drive *Bonzo Bear* forward with its 14 ft diameter load, it was plentiful in comparison to the room available to get it on to the Cometto load carrier. If getting out of the mountain was bad enough, Miller then had to tranship the drum on to a smaller low loader before they were allowed to road haul the load to South Wales for storage

John Angles is at the wheel of
Econofreight's 300PT Fiat 6×4
tractor pictured in Park Street,
Bristol during 1982 starting up the
1 in 8 gradient. The left-hand drive
Fiat was originally operated by Albin
Von Bogert of Belgium under the
banner of VBA Trucking, Antwerp.
The 70 tonne pedestal crane,
supported on the Nicolas semi-
trailer built by Stothert and Pitt, is
being hauled from Bath to
Avonmouth docks. This weight is
well within the design capacity of
the Fiat which is now rated for 180
tonnes GTW operation. Following in
convoy is NPY 439P hauling a
similar load also destined for a
North Sea oil rig

18

Left The two-bed four Nicolas hydraulically suspended semi-trailer was an innovative if somewhat expensive method of getting heavier all up weights out of your articulated load carrier. Margaret Lambert of Richmond's Studio 5 was on hand to record the first load hauled on Geoff Johnson's big Nic as it arrived in Scorton Quarry, North Yorkshire having hauled this RB machine from Harrogate in August 1981. All up weight, excluding the leaning John Allison, of the combination was in excess of 100 tonnes. The Scania 141 tractor JPT 199T was well liked by Johnson although they upset its manufacturer slightly by replacing

the original gearbox with a 15-speed Fuller unit. At the time of writing the Scania had just left the Johnson fleet having been replaced by a heavier specification DAF 3300

Below Left Hallett Silbermann's senior driver John Macklin was at the wheel of this 110 tonne rated Volvo F12 coupled to a 100 tonne capacity Broshius during September 1983 when the outfit hauled this 60 tonne pontoon from Cardiff to South Shields. At 19 ft wide the owners of the load, Christiani and Nielsen, had to assure the Department of Transport that it was urgently required for specialist marine work up in the north east

before permission to move by road was given. Even with a police escort chauffeur Macklin still had an interesting 400 mile journey which included traversing the contraflow system on the M50 where it crossed the River Severn at 3 am on a Saturday morning. John also took the pontoon through the Tyne Tunnel twice as routing staff were informed initially that its destination was at the other side of the Tyne in North Shields

Below Right CAJ 357Y is one of the latest DAF 3300s operated by Econofreight and driver Bill Johnson is seen putting the 150 tonne GTW rating of the 6×4

tractor to the test as it climbs the 1 in 10 Billingham Bank with a 90 tonne boiler section. The load was road hauled from Hartlepool docks *en route* from its manufacturers in Paris, France being part of the new nitric acid plant being constructed at ICI Billingham. The semi-trailer is of Nicolas construction although its red colouring gives away the fact that it was on hire from GCS Johnson of Barton. The blue power pack carried over the trailer's leading two axles is Econofreight's own, carried as a back up intended for the 'just in case' situation. The 300 PT at the bottom of the bank is carrying a similar load on the same journey

Above Leicester Heavy Haulage of Loughborough have shown great allegiance to the ERF marque for some considerable time having operated most of their standard machines at one time or another. NUT 345W is by no means a regular production option, it being rated to operate up to 170 tonnes GTW. With a rear bogie capable of supporting a total of nearly 36 tonnes, the Cummins engined tractor is more than capable of supporting terrific weights when operated in articulated form. It is pictured on one of its early jobs hauling a stator set *en route* to Liverpool docks. The hydraulically suspended modular trailer is of Cometto manufacture being two four-row bogies coupled together to give ample support for the 95 tonne load

Right UEF 728X is seen backing on to the *TOR Anglia* in Immingham Docks in February 1984. The 14 ft wide load has just been hauled from Queensferry, North Wales, the outfit's all up weight being 57 tonnes. The load was taken right through to its destination in Holland by driver Gordon Wragg. Supporting the weight is trailer number 930, a hard worked King tri-axle unit. Econofreight well like DAF machines having used both the four-wheeled and six-wheeled tractors for this weight band since 1976

Above The Class 40 locomotive still makes a major contribution in hauling British Rail rolling stock although 40106 was reportedly the first of its type to go into service on a preserved railway. Gerald Bowden purchased this machine on behalf of Great Central Railway (1976) Ltd during 1983 but it had to stand a year before a route and method of movement could be devised. Leicester Heavy Haulage moved the 128 tonnes of locomotive during June 1984 although weight limitations ruled out delivering the mass at the normal slip off point of Quorn. Loading was also memorable with the daylight spent jacking it up on girders, which saved £4000 on craning, then Don Moore nosed the extended eight-row Cometto trailer underneath with only the light of a car's headlamps into precisely the right position on his first push. Driver Moore then circumnavigated Loughborough, reversed half a mile down Wharncliffe Road but only managed to reach Grand Central's premises by driving into his own depot and through a gap in the perimeter fence

Right During August 1983 Sunter-ITM moved four of these dock cranes when it was decided to relocate them between the Alexandra and King George docks in Hull. There have been taller cranes than this moved in one piece

but these 128 tonne monsters were hauled a lengthy 1.5 miles on a round the docks route. With a centre of gravity 51 ft above the ground, carriage had to be particularly delicate especially when a gradient of 1 in 29 had to be traversed. The two hauling tractors were Volvo RDC 319X and Titan EJW 229V driven by Alan Massey and Malcolm Johnson respectively, both machines being fitted with torque converters

In the early 1980s plans were made to redevelop the under-used Preston docks into a high quality marina. One of the early jobs was to remove, refurbish and then relocate a pair of dock gates. The combined efforts of J. D. White's T300 Liebherr telescopic crane with Barry Banfield at the controls lifted this gate out of the water on Thursday 14 June 1984. Chris Miller's Mack and Thornycroft with their respective drivers Peter Beasley and Tony Scott using Cometto running gear were then needed to track the gate down into a horizontal position to rest on Miller's infamous tubs. The two five-row bogies were then coupled up to form a ten-line unit and with *Bonzo Bear* taking the strain, the 110 tonnes or so of gate was moved across the dock to its refurbishing position

Below The camera isn't lying, those two rows of axles are in mid air. One of the many attributes of the hydraulically suspended modular trailer is that with the turning of certain taps, the wheels can be locked into position so that even though the ground may disappear the suspension doesn't collapse. This situation developed as the Nicolas load carrier had to be placed in position once the power jacks had lifted the crane clear. Operations superintendent is the white-overalled Charlie Hynd and although ITM may describe this operation as fairly routine, it is the ability to perform such miracles which keeps them in business

Above Right RDC 318X does not bear any distinctive manufacturer badges and on its arrival in the United Kingdom it did create a problem for enthusiasts to establish what it was. The machine is a combination of the best bits and pieces assembled by the French company of Nicolas who are probably better known for their

hydraulic modular trailers. Sunter's model is the TR66C4C which has a Cummins KTA 450 supercharged diesel engine. The drive is taken through a Clark torque converter to a Clark eight-speed gearbox with 'powershift' operation. All three Soma axles are driven and Michelin tyres fitted all round. At 9 ft 10 in. wide the Tractomas is bigger than some although the front wheels are slightly inboard and its track is 7 ft 9 in. It is by no means perfect but all who have seen it at work know that it is quite a machine

Below Right 26 February 1984 at 9.30 am was damp and miserable in Brenda Road at Hartlepool. At 37 ft 6 in. high this 190 tonne Foster Wheeler package boiler was one of three similar loads that the Fisher boats were to ro-ro across the North Sea. Hartlepool is well used to seeing these massive loads so on such an inclement day it was not surprising that the only spectator in this Cyril Hull photograph is the author who is absorbing the sight, sound and smell of the day. Even trailerman John Garrett has climbed up into the dry of the Tractomas cab alongside driver Albert Lowes leaving pom-pom hated Jack Higgins to walk in the wet. The following Volvo driven by Alan Massey double headed the French tractor over the acute Newburn bridge whilst last in line is Peter Clemmett driving YVN 308T hauling an Economiser which is positively light at 66 tonnes. Both the load carriers had a reverse of half a mile ahead of them from Church Street into the docks as turning room at the roll-on, roll-off quay is particularly limited

ICI Agricultural Division   Protein Plant

2
Long time passing

23 February 1978 was quite a day for Rigging
International for the transportation and later erection of
this 632 Fermenter column were to win them the Rigging
Award of the Year, an important American trophy.
Originally the haul was planned to utilize Sunters' Nicolas
modular trailers but in the end two, 500 tonne capacity
crawlers piloted by Dieter Wilmaser and Ken Hodgson
under superintendent Alf Waller did the cross country
haul. This column was the maiden load for the *Starman
Anglia* which had one of its forward funnels removed to
provide ample internal space. Anxiety was created over
the state of the tide for on the day the ship came into
Bamletts Wharf the water was 3 ft higher than expected.
A specially prepared road had been laid down for
crawlers which included the crossing of the public
Haverton Hill Road and Belasis Avenue

Above Mick Crowshaw is at the wheel of TSL's faithful F89 which is seen leaving the premises of Adamson and Hatchett at Dukinfield with a 120 tonne column that was hauled to Liverpool docks prior to its sea journey to Sullom Voe. The Volvo tractor performed ten years of hard work for TSL but the most memorable part of this job was that it was the first big outing for the ten rows of Goldhoffer axles. George Curtis had been rather disappointed when one manufacturer rejected his order and returned his deposit so he set out into Europe in search of two five-row bogies that could work as a ten-row unit, his travels taking

him to Menningham where he knocked on the door of Goldhoffers

Above Right The company of Planthaul used to specialize in long distance continental heavy haulage but when project manager Dave Alderson was asked to supervise the movement of eight items of refinery equipment from Italy to Milford Haven, it soon became apparent that overland road transport was not the most practical or economic. Road hauled from Bergarmo to Porto Marghera by the Italian company Delta Transport, the items were then loaded on to the *Fairmast*. The ship discharged its

load at Pembroke dock and included in the entourage of vehicles used to complete the journey was J. B. Rawcliffe's well turned out 150 tonne capacity Mack ACK 645V. Seen leaving the docks, the 6×4 tractor is coupled to a 60 ft Transquip extendable trailer which sported a steerable rear bogie. The odd looking bridgework at the rear of the 46 tonne vessel was to give temporary support to the load which was close to 80 ft long

Right Econofreight's Fiat FAJ 299V is seen in the premises of British Croyplant, Edmonton nose pinned

to a four-bed six Nicolas load
carrier. The outfit has just pulled this
65 tonne cold box out from the
construction shop which was
packaged in that particular manner
to ensure it could get through the
door. Once in the open air cranes of
Stanley Davies rotated the box end
to end then turned it on its side
prior to leaving for London docks.
At 96 ft long and 15 ft 8 in. high
the move required careful route
planning and rigorous checking

Above This is one of two similar columns that Econofreight moved from Grosvenor Steel, Manchester to the Shell refinery at Stanlow in October 1983. Even getting out of the works required the removal of a stretch of fencing but the laid down route for this job saw the pulling Volvo virtually circumnavigating Manchester rather than heading directly into Cheshire. Very shallow supporting saddles were used to take the 14 ft 9 in. diameter load so that the running height would allow it to get under motorway bridges. The length of this column was just on 100 ft and its weight approximately 50 tonnes

Left The ingredients of concrete when separated are fairly innocuous but mixed together they produce some of the most awkward loads regularly moved by the heavy haulier. Beams of 90 ft like this Dow Mac load hauled from Eaglescliffe to Derby during 1982 require supporting at their extreme ends and are normally hauled utilizing an independent bogie. G. E. Stiller of Darlington demonstrate an alternative, arguably more safe method to the floating bogie, with a well turned out extendable Nooteboom semi-trailer. With a capacity of 70 tonnes it has strength enough for its 54 tonne load. DAF tractor unit PFL 958R was originally operated by Dow Mac of Tallington near Stamford before being sold to Stiller

Above In these days of highly
sophisticated modular bogies which
offer all wheel steering at the flick of
a switch or pull of a lever through a
maze of hydraulic pipes, it is still
worth remembering that the way in
which a long load is manoeuvred is
still a matter of choice. It is a lot
cheaper to use a modified six-
wheeler which is perhaps past its
best and many an Albion Riever has
ended its days in this form. Hills of
Botley have a reputation of getting
the best from their diverse
equipment and they are seen
manoeuvring this 98 ft long, 35-
tonne cracker plant in the Esso

Fawley plant during the summer of 1980. Roy Wiseman is steering the Guy Big J which lacks its engine and cab whilst Bob Bernard is at the helm of the pulling Scammell Crusader SNB 413J

Left The directions given to driver Ernie Pickersgill would have read fairly simply 'turn left at the traffic lights'. The fact that he is leaving Head Wrightson's Thornaby works with yet another massive load didn't effect the instructions although the time taken to complete the turn was perhaps longer than some although the outfit was 145 ft long. This was

the second of two coke drums moved by Ernie so he had in fact put in some practice with the first and did manage to clear these lights without bursting a tyre on the ornamental footpath close to his offside. At an all up 336 tonnes the Scammell performed without fault with the most noise coming from the clang of the radiator shutters rather than the murmur of the Cummins engine

Above Right At 155 ft 10 in. long, this glass-lined pipe was at the time of the haul, November 1983, the longest load ever to pass through

the Tyne Tunnel. Mick Crowshaw is at the wheel of George Curtis's hard worked Scania 142E whilst the 54 tonne pipe is supported on two five-axle Goldhoffer bogies. The move under the River Tyne cost the Epworth operator £500 for the exclusive use of the two-way stretch of roadway although what was thought might be the most difficult part of the Coalville to Wallsend journey passed off without incident in less than 25 minutes

Left Substantial development has been made in the field of mobile craneage but their utilization can be expensive so sometimes a haulier endeavours to make the best of the resources he has at hand thus saving on cost. Unloading this 173 ft long stacker reactor column at Ellesmere Port on Boxing Day 1983 found that the geography of the situation just wouldn't allow the heavy lift ship *Happy Mammoth* to swing the load straight on to the waiting bogies. Econofreight's answer was to first support the 245 tonne load on the leading bogie and gently draw it away as the ship's crane held the rear of the column. Photographed here, the second bogie has been pushed underneath the rear of the load and final checks are being made before the slings are unhitched and the Nicolas axles take all the weight as the load is moved towards the Shell refinery at Stanlow

Following Page Mid-morning Tuesday 27 December 1983 found Ernie Pickersgill piloting XTM 546X round the junction of Lower Mersey Street and Dock Street, Ellesmere Port with what some people believed was the heaviest load ever to pass through the town. The excessive front overhang was brought about because the predetermined front carrying point was well down the 173 ft length. The seven mile haul to Stanlow took just over four hours, a relatively short period when you learn that the journey for this 245 tonne, 15 ft 8 in. diameter column commenced in Japan. A particularly interesting part of this heavy haul was that a fortnight earlier Econofreight had hauled 200 tonnes of crane ballast round the proposed route inside the Shell refinery as a dry run just to ensure that the internal road surface could withstand the heavy loading

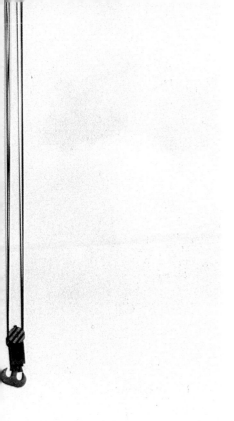

Anyone coming down Vulcan Street, Middlesbrough during the early part of 1983 may have had the good fortune to witness this monster creeping across their path prior to a three-point turn to pull close alongside Vulcan Quay. As one of two floatation tanks, it was built under cover in Head Wrightson's Vulcan works for a Norwegian sector riser platform. Each load was 16 ft in diameter and from tip to toe was 208 ft long but an all up weight in excess of 300 tonnes still seemed easy meat for UVN 44S. Eagle-eyed observers will note the lack of elasticated air lines running between the two bogies but to save time in rigging, the Volvo F89 tractor ran alongside the rear bogie it being piped in to do the braking as and when required

Right Some people describe Sunters' Tractomas as ugly but as any good photographer will tell you the lighting can make all the difference. For the night of Saturday 24 March the outfit stood bathed in floodlights to allow any would-be spectators just to admire. The offices of Head Wrightson look down on what might have been their swan song for at the time of the haul they seemed destined for closure. Many a mountain-type load has passed along this frontage although some of Head's most famous loads, the Bradwell boilers, were launched out the back gate and floated down the River Tees

Below Saturday 24 March 1984 saw Albert Lowes easing ever so gently out of the gateway of Head Wrightson on to Trafalgar Street, Thornaby. For 48 weeks this 304 tonnes of stainless steel had been cossetted in the dry but as it was pulled out of the construction shop for the first time the heavens opened on load and onlookers alike. It took just over an hour to move 100 yards but doing this sideways shuffle was not easy and the Sunter men were well pleased with their progress. Front bogie steersman was John Wood who is getting in some practice of walking backwards. The next day he was to walk $5\frac{1}{2}$ miles nearly all in this fashion

Above Sunday 25 March 1984 dawned clear and bright
with the slight frost only of concern to the spectators.
6.40 am saw Mr Lowes climbing ever so slowly on to
Victoria Bridge at Thornaby with little regard for the red
traffic lights. This junction is of a normal crossroads-type
construction but to allow right turning loads like this to
escape from Head Wrightsons, a special ramp was built
to cut the corner off. The 18.9 litres of Cummins engine
in the Nicolas tractor was hardly above a murmur but all
in the vicinity of the load were deafened by the small
power packs used on the trailer for suspension and
steering

Right Photographer Mike Brown had to climb 11 flights
of stairs on an adjacent high rise block of flats to get this
221 ft 2 in. of load into proper perspective. Some of the
street furniture which was removed is shown in the shot
but the Tyne Tees Television vehicles at the top of the
photograph were not on hand to film this momentous
occasion they being there to record a more regular event
at the nearby place of worship later in the day

8.10 am, Sunday 25 March saw
four members of the load's police
escort line abreast Norton Road
whilst Mr Lowes and the long load
creeps ever onwards. Left to right
are Constable Malcolm Wilson
astride a Suzuki GS1100; Inspector
Barry Monkman GS1000; Sergeant
John Tindale GS1100 and Constable
Alan Baines GS1000. The Suzukis
are reckoned to have a top speed of
135 mph although with the
impediments of their equipment in
police form, their top speed is
reduced to about 115 mph

Above To me this photograph shows what heavy haulage is really all about. It took Econofreight's staff eight months to sort a route for the transportation of three rotary kilns from New Dunford Engineering, Doncaster to ICI Runcorn. The kilns measured 62 ft long and at 147 tonnes a time seem an ideal fit for the 9 ft 8 in. wide 14-row Nicolas trailers. Heading this duo is John Angles driving the F12 whilst Ernie Pickersgill follows at the helm of Scammel S24 XTM 546X, the outfits pictured on Penistone Road, Sheffield, in February 1984. In reserve was the fleet's N10, RDC 955X, which was used for double heading over the Pennines

Right Proudly proclaiming its dimensions, the first of the three Littlebrook boilers is seen as its resting place is under construction. The '251 tonne, 106 ft 6 in.' long vessel was hauled by Wynns from Wolverhampton to the Pomona dock in Manchester where it was pushed onboard the ro-ro ship *Kingsnorth Fisher*. Rolled off at the quay adjoining Kingsnorth power station, Wynns tractors hitched back up to complete the journey to site. The odd configuration of 17 axles was prompted by the Cheshire highway authorities who asked for an additional three axles to the originally proposed 14. The first boiler was unloaded into storage for close on a year before Wynns moved it in doors into the power station proper

3 King Contractor

GEC Larne may have apologized for any inconvenience to other road users, but they were more than pleased with having manufactured this and three other similar vessels destined for California in December 1977. Magnaload's Contractor TRL 924H and Volvo F89 NPY 439P, plus Northern Ireland Carriers larger Contractor XUP 999F, were involved in the 25 mile road haul to Belfast docks for the first three loads although at one point the hauling tractors were unhitched as the 401 tonnes of vessel and 16 rows of heavy-duty Scheuerle running gear were winched over a rather delicate road bridge. At this time this was the heaviest load carried on roads in Great Britain

Above During October 1974 Wynns supplied the final link in a journey which took these two reactor vessels almost half way round the world. Constructed in Japan, the transportation company Big Lift provided the sea travel whilst a special quay had been constructed at Stanlow that would take the shallow draft of this barge right into the heart of the refinery. Positioning the rear of the two bogies which had to be pushed underneath can be particularly awkward when no form of winching can be provided from the other end. Wynns' answer was to push the first bogie under as far as possible, then insert a drawbar link to the next bogie and push that one under until the rearmost one was in the required position

Left At 150 ft long this box girder was obliged to take up more than its fair share of the roadway as it crosses the River Aire *en route* from Keighley to Immingham. At the time this was the largest crane to be built by the Keighley crane manufacturer John Smith, and was for delivery to Norway's biggest steelworks in Oslo. Michael Albone is at the wheel of LFB 716K which rather significantly started life with Sparrow who specialize in cranes of a different nature. One of the biggest problems found by the Watkinson's crew was getting out of Smith's and that was only achieved by using Cometto all wheel steering bogies plus removing the perimeter fence of Magnet Joinery whose premises are located opposite the Smith's factory doorway

Above Left and Left Challenger with Bill Wade at the wheel provided the propulsion off the barge and the round the site haul of no more than two miles for these 285 tonne lumps whilst *Conqueror* is seen at the rear in reserve. Loading on to the two ten-row Nicolas bogies was made a lot easier because the supporting saddles had been manufactured as part of the vessel, these also assisting for the unloading at their storage point on to large concrete stools. With the arrival of the second consignment in May 1975, Sid Davies in *Conqueror* flexed his muscles with a column slightly longer than the reactors but not quite as heavy

Above The local authority in charge of highways in Renfrew has always shown great consideration in the building of roads that lead from the premises of Babcock Power Ltd for they realize that the dimensions of some of their exports are not always suitable to follow the same path as any other normal motorist. Pickfords' M5037 is using the special, heavy load route which bisects the roundabout in Glebe Street as the outfit makes its way to King George V dock in Glasgow on 28 September 1979. The 212 tonne converter was one of four built by Babcock for Davy Powergas, their eventual destination being Techmashimpost in the USSR. SYO 400F was one of the second phase of 240 tonne GTW Contractors bought by Pickfords in the mid-1960s. Nicolas heavyweight axles are supporting the load and it is not a trick of the light that the leading four rows are a different colour to the rearmost eight

Above 1 November 1978 saw Peter Clemmett keeping right of the keep left bollards as he eases Sunters' NAJ 103P out of Trafalger Street, Thornaby. The 132 tonnes of secondary reformer was eventually destined for Indonesia but on this particular day it was only taken less than a mile down the road to the premises of J. D. White where it was to be stored for close on 18 months. The biggest difficulty in carrying this vessel was that its structure made it act like a self-righting skittle. In fact when the securing chains were released the front lifted itself off the packing which meant the balance on the Nicolas was particularly delicate

Left In their time Pickfords have limbo'd underneath quite a few different structures but to negotiate the NCB Immingham bulk terminal conveyor during May 1979 with this Foster Wheeler waste heat boiler, something more drastic had to be done. Birtley Engineering Co and Kramo Montage (UK) Ltd were responsible for the lifting/lowering of the roadway protection span and as time meant a great deal of money in this instance, the operation was done under a particularly critical schedule. Destined for the Lindsey Oil Refinery at South Killingholme, the 240 tonne, 28 ft wide boiler had been built in Hartlepool then shipped down to Immingham docks on board the *Starman Anglia*. Pickfords utilized 11 rows of Nicolas running gear whilst Scammell PGO 712E is doing the pulling with Mk II Contractor XUU 925T, less than a month old, up ahead in reserve

Left True perspective is given to this massive pipe rack which was one of 37 similar loads hauled by Sunter-ITM from the mainland of Great Britain up to the oil terminal at Sullom Voe. NAJ 103P was the only one of the four Sunters Contractors to be named, *Fearnought* originally being transferred from an army tank on to the Rotinoff. With the Atlantic retiring in 1976, driver Peter Clemmett transferred the name to his then new Scammell although had Wynns not used it before, he would of preferred the title of *Dreadnought* to describe his heavyweight mount

Above To emphasize the connection between ITM and Sunters, during the early part of 1983 all the latter's four big Contractors received a repaint which suggested to some that the vehicles had in fact been sold. This was not the case although the paint job was thought by many not to be as good as the one it replaced. Both styles can be seen here as Bill Jamieson in LAJ 798P heads up Albert Lowes in RDC 318X, the outfits having just left the premises of Foster Wheeler on Brenda Road, Hartlepool. At close to 120 tonnes these boilers were relatively light although they had an impressive width of 18 ft 9 in. and height of 27 ft 11 in. Conveyed to the local docks their eventual destination was Haldor Topsoe, Bombay

Below During August 1981 Pickfords' Glasgow depot was involved in a particularly tricky job bringing these five loads across the sea wall at Killingholme and then delivering them to the Lindsey Oil Refinery. With dimensions of 140 ft long, 33 ft wide, 50 ft high and near 270 tonnes in weight branch manager Jim Parkinson had to worry about contact between these loads and the sea wall. The barge from United Towing of Hull also had to be securely tied down for even in heavily ballasted form, it endeavoured to slide away down the greasy foreshore after beaching. The loads were all moved on Nicolas running gear, they all being loaded on the barge by using the in-built hydraulics of the trailers. This Geoffrey Pass photograph shows that Pickfords used three Contractors for the job. The double-headed pair had more than enough power for the climb on to drier land but Pickfords preferred to ease them up by winch and so not risk the massive tractive effort disturbing the bridging ramp over the delicate wall. Unloaded at the refinery, Pickfords gang used skid pads on beams to slide the modules into their final resting position

Above Pickfords Heavy Haulage of Glasgow moved three of these 340 tonne steam drums into the new Drax power station over a period of three years ending in May 1983. Quite some weight for XUU 919T hauling 16 rows of Nicolas axles although the road haul from Babcock Power at Renfrew to Yorkshire was augmented by a ride on one of the Fisher boats from Glasgow dock to the slip off point adjacent to the power station. The well turned out M9530 with David Ginn at the wheel was Pickfords first Mk II Contractor which sported an Allison automatic gearbox driven by a Cummins 450 power pack. This drum was moved twice by Pickfords, first it was unloaded into a storage point, then a few months later it was moved into the power station proper

Left Bill Jamieson at the wheel of LAJ 798P is pulling the same construction as Jimmy Goulding but due to the manoeuvring on site the load is now being pulled in the opposite direction. Sunters used Nicolas running gear to take the weight but rigged the 19 ft 8 in. wide trailer in four-file wide configuration which meant it had 16 tyres on each of its 12 rows of axles. Even with all-wheel steering the load had to be slewed through one gap which even by Sunters' modest terms was described as tight. To clear walls and other similar obstructions adjacent to the route, a great deal of packing had to be utilized to give adequate clearance. The piece was part of a semi-submersible drilling rig being built for Dome Petroleum of Canada

Left Davy McKee may have won the contract but it was Pickfords Industrial who accepted the challenge and utilized their Mk II Contractors to move this, the first of four massive 325 tonne castings from Doncaster to Sheffield during January 1983. XUU 919T and XUU 925T may have left the Scammell factory in identical form but the pride which driver David Ginn has in its appearance reflects on the immaculate condition that the former vehicle is turned out. Trundling about with this monster, Pickfords had to keep to a very strict timetable and they are seen leaving Doncaster on a Thursday afternoon as this was early closing day. The yellow Selwood power pack resting on the top left of 919's ballast box was to provide ample air for braking on the Nicolas 12 ft wide trailer, whilst next to it is a Volkswagen-engined power pack which energized the sophisticated hydraulic suspension and steering throughout its 213 ft length

Below Pickfords had no choice but to use the M18 and M1 as part of their route although in doing so they had to accede to the highway authorities demands that the maximum axle loading on the outfit was not to exceed 18 tonnes. The roadtrain left Doncaster using only 16 axles but once it reached the M18 the police escort took it down the slip road, through a gap in the central reservation and then it reversed back underneath the intersection flyover. Here the Pickfords men spent all Friday, as they weren't allowed to move until first light Saturday, to add the additional eight axles. Gavin Dempsey is pictured heading up David Ginn with 10.5 in. deflection in the trailer spread as they head south for Junction 31 where once again the central reservation was crossed

Dock Express Shipping of Rotterdam operate amongst their diverse fleet four very special ships although rather unromantically they follow the practice of barge operators of being numbered rather than named. Dock Express 12, sister ship to Dock Express 10 and 11,

was built by Verolme Schoopswerf Heusden, Holland being completed in October 1979. Most distinctive part of their appearance are the travelling crane gantries which in unison can lift 1000 tonnes, although the latest Dock Express 20 can lift 1200 tonnes on its pair.

Developing 8500 bhp, the two Stork-Werkspoor diesel engines can propel the 6905 tonnes of deadweight up to a steady 16 knots. Seen operating as a normal self-contained cargo ship, the 490 ft long Dock Express can also work as a roll-on, roll-off vessel but more

importantly has a semi-submersible feature of being able to sink itself marginally to allow its cargo to float off where necessary

When the Dock Express comes to town it is a matter of working round the clock to unload. The Pickfords crew appreciated that this cargo just in from Japan had arrived at RGC-UIE, Methil in the July of 1982, rather than the depths of a Scottish winter. David Ginn and Gavin Dempsey driving the Mk II Contractors had to distribute these massive fabrications at various parts around the site, as they in turn would take up a very small part of a gigantic oil rig being constructed. Nicolas running gear was utilized in relatively normal 16-row units to carry the 406 tonnes of buoyancy tubes. For the heavier 535 tonne flotation tanks and the 504 tonnes of lower bottle sections, which resembled the inside of a revolver, Pickfords used a four-file wide Nicolas and two-load spreaders to take the strain

4
The strength of girders

For many years Pickfords have got great service from the varying type of girder trailer produced by Cranes of Norfolk. 1520 offered a capacity of 110 tonnes on its eight rather small axles, the rearmost bogie being steered automatically as the main frame girders turned to follow the pulling tractor. To independently manoeuvre these rear wheels, however, using the small donkey engine, the steering rod had first to be manually disconnected. The engine power also provided 15 in. of stroke on the main

trailer king post to assist if the load had to be lifted or lowered. The outfit is pictured close to Loch Ness about 1974 being headed up by WGC 638G, a Contractor rated for 123 tonnes gross operation. Driver Jimmy Hendrie is taking this 60 tonne, 16 ft diameter ring to the Northern Scotland Hydro Electric Board plant at Foyens

The Air Cushion Equipment developed by the British Hovercraft Corporation in association with the Central Electricity Generating Board proved to be a massive step forward in the movement of large generators and transformers about the country. Their concealed mass of weight, sometimes in excess of 300 tonnes, would have dictated that numerous bridges would have required rebuilding before they could have taken the weight. In fact, it was calculated that for the first hundred loads that utilized the equipment, in excess of £4,000,000 was saved in rebuilding costs as the ACE blew over a thousand bridge crossings. The Wynns' outfit is pictured in December 1975 on one of their many Stafford–Manchester runs relieving weight on road surfaces in Cheshire

Above Wynns Heavy Haulage were involved in the first operation of the Air Cushion Equipment when a 157 tonne AEI transformer was blown across the Felin Puleston bridge *en route* to Legacy, mid Wales during April 1967. Nine years on they are pictured south of Manchester with 195 *Resolute* coupled up to Nicolas girder trailer 987 with the cushion equipment receiving attention. One of the drawbacks of the Series 1 version of the ACE was that the pushing tractor, on this occasion *Dreadnought* had to be disconnected from the roadtrain to allow the trusty Rootes blower vehicle to hook itself on behind. Inside that vehicle were housed the four turbines which could generate relief that would support approximately one third of the trailer's gross weight

Opposite Page and Following Developed in modular form, the Series 2 Air Cushion Equipment proved to be less bulky yet far more efficient than its Series 1 predecessor. The four units, comprising of a flexible skirt, air supply units and fuel tank modules, ducting and pressure regulating system plus controls and instruments are pictured attached to Pickfords Crane Fruehauf trailer TM1277 as it approaches Ince power station, Ellesmere Port in June 1976. The ACE is particularly effective for bridges which have simply supported spans of up to 50 ft and Scammell M4847 NYE 593E is seen easing over a bridge which the vast majority of motorists just wouldn't realize was there. Power is provided by four Noel Penny turbines although only three are used for relief, the fourth acting as a standby unit and discharging its air to the atmosphere through the control system. On this particular job the Pickfords men had the luxury of being able to drive straight over the plinth, which meant they could unload *in situ* rather than having to winch, skid and drag their load from where they are obliged to deposit it

Serving the far flung outposts of the electrical industry means the transformer trains and core carriers are seen regularly in some strange places. On 22 May 1977 Robert Price recorded this move of a 125-tonne Parson transformer after it had rolled off in Penzance docks. Bill Wade is at the wheel of 196 *Talisman* as he twists Crane girder trailer 999 round the impressive frontage of Lloyds Bank in the heart of the town with 183 pushing from the rear. *En route* to the Indian Queens sub station, the Series 1 version of the Air Cushion Equipment was utilized and is seen blowing as it crosses a railway bridge at Hoyle. The most memorable aspect of this move for the Wynns' staff was that it was the last job for the 300 tonne capacity Crane girder trailer before it was sold overseas

Previous Page The big girder trailer outfit is a very impressive sight wherever it goes for even in unladen condition the 300 tonne capacity Crane Fruehauf load carriers tip the scales at close to 80 tonnes. Cranes of Dereham originally cornered this select market although now they tend to concentrate on more routine types of trailer. This CEGB photograph shows the roadtrain headed up by NYE 593E as it approaches the Dinorwic pumped storage station in North Wales with one of seven 275 tonne Parsons Peebles transformers. Shipped between Granton and Port Penrhyn, Pickfords had to take six of them down the Dinorwic tunnels to the main gallery. The girder trailer can be seen to have a bolster packing block in its suspension so that an extra foot of daylight can be utilized to clear a vicious hump on the road haul to site

Right Situations are encountered by the exceptionally heavy haulier when no matter how many wheels that are put under a load or how hard the air cushion equipment is blown, the road surface still isn't strong enough to take the weight. One method to round this dilemma is to use the CEGB bridging raft which as its name implies, is able to bridge across a weak stretch of roadway. Wynns Contractor 281 is seen climbing up on to the raft *en route* from Lowestoft to Great Yarmouth as gangman Pete Hodge looks on. The girder trailer being used is the faithful Crane 1001, a unit which has more than earned its keep since it came from Dereham in 1963 as the first 300 tonne capacity trailer in the land

Left A regular lunchtime sight in Stafford is watching the impressive girder trailers leaving the GEC works and turning on to the A34 Lichfield Road with yet another export order. Wrekin's WR50 is seen in 1981 supporting a 220 tonne transformer destined for installation in the Castle Peak power station at Hong Kong. At the time of purchase WR50 was a version of the new lightweight girder trailer having 14 axles and a capacity of 260 tonnes. Wrekin Roadways were bought by the BUT group and their livery was eventually dropped, the vehicles being repainted in Wynns' colours.

This Nicolas trailer was one of the load carriers sold to GEC Distribution Services Division although Wynns continued to provide propulsion and servicing of these lengthy load carriers

Below Left Robert Price observed Wrekin Roadways' *Invader* stopping the traffic on London's North Circular during 1980 as minor adjustments are made to the street furniture to allow the 19 ft of girth a trouble free passage. At the time the 185 tonnes of transformer was one of the heaviest loads to travel through the metropolis. The load

had originated from Liverpool and was *en route* to the Willesden sub station on board WR1, Wrekins' first 14-axle girder trailer. The haul went off without incident although I have been asked not to comment about the length of time spent jacking this off at the unload point

Below Right Bill Sadler is at the wheel of Wynns' *Invincible* DBO 661V, fleet number 640, the second of the Mk II Contractors bought by this company. He is pictured crossing Hartford bridge, Northwich, Cheshire in this CEGB photograph with a 120 tonne transformer that

was hauled from Connahs Quay, Deeside to Rochdale in May 1980. The girder trailer is again the Crane, fleet number 1001. This particular unit has served Wynns well since it came although new running gear has been recently fitted. The original equipment comprised two six-row bogies which comprised a four-row and a two-row coupled together. The new equipment is of straight six-rows which although similar to the original equipment, these bogies can be used independently of the main girder frame

Above You can't say that the Wynns-GEC contract outfit is nothing if not distinctive be it inching out of Stafford or traversing the veldt of North Kent. Painted black to specifically match GEC's trailers are Wynns' Scammells XFA 217X and WNT 307S although this complete outfit really originates from the fleet of Wrekin Roadways. The Nicolas girder trailer took the designation WR100 when it came to Telford and at 125 tonnes empty it was at the time the largest girder trailer in the country. WNT 307S was well known in Wrekins' colours although XFA 217X was stored for some considerable time before coming on to the road in the then amalgamated Wynns/Wrekin fleet

Left The culmination of several years planning is seen in this Devon and Cornwall Constabulary photograph taken by Sergeant Hext at 11 am on Sunday 22 October 1983 on the A30, Exeter's eastern by-pass. It took that length of time plus over half a million pounds spent in road improvements for the CEGB to arrange with the various authorities for the transportation of the 152 tonne Hawker Siddeley transformer from Teignmouth to Alverdiscott. Roger Colcombe is at the helm of the Wynns leading tractor DBF 134Y, whilst at the wheel of the following police Range Rover is Constable Alan Down. Reportedly the largest load to travel through this police force area, the roadtrain's vital statistics were 210 ft overall length, 350 tonnes combination weight, 17 ft wide and 19 ft high

Grain generating station is perched on the end of the Isle of Grain midway between the Rivers Thames and Medway. Nearest roll off point for the massive girder trailer outfit is Kingsnorth power station so it is ten miles of fairly rural running for the Wynns' crews to their destination. CEGB photographer David Shaw recorded the passage of this stator core on 27 April 1984 and his excellent photographs show how flexible the suspension on the trailer has to be to negotiate the occasional tight turn. The residents of Stoke have grown used to seeing this load carriage although its passage still demands that you stop and stare

Above Left At 245 ft from tip to toe this girder trailer outfit, even with all-wheel steering still requires a different form of manoeuvring and although drivers Ron Savage and Mick Naggington do look as though they are playing a tug of war, they form up in this manner to ease the 254 tonnes of load into the exact position inside the station. Either heading backwards or forwards it still means that the 463 tonnes all up weight has a pilot looking and driving the way it is going

Left Unless you have connections with the south-east of England, Sellindge may not mean a great deal but for people in the electricity supply industry this place has just as much exciting significance as perhaps even Dinorwic. From this site in Kent, electricity will be either sent to or received from France, being converted for use in the relevant country. The contract also means a great deal of work for the heavy haulier for at 325 tonnes these NEI transformers are the

heaviest yet produced in this country. The Wynns' roadtrains have an all up weight close to 500 tonnes so the loads are ro-ro'd into Folkestone prior to delivery to site. Roger Colcombe is the leading driver of the outfit which is pictured in this CEGB photograph in June 1984 having just left the M20 via a specially-built slip road only used for the delivery of abnormal loads, approximately 1 mile from site. 126 as Wynns' enthusiasts will know is RWO 73R, *Superior* and the girder trailer used on this occasion is a Wynns' special being Nicolas axles and Cometto girders

Above Right Tony Swan is seen with trailerman Billy Thew in the premises of Head Wrightson (Teesdale) Ltd about to leave Thornaby for yet another five-day round trip to northern Scotland. Their load is one of 82 cell shells, 33 ft 7 in. long, 15 ft high and 5 ft 8 in. wide weighing 27 tonnes that Sunters delivered during 1979 and 1980 to the British Aluminium

Lochaber smelter modernization plant at Fort William. Five sets of these special girder trailers were built and as can be seen they were normally carried resting on 6 in. of timber. At Crianlarrich and Balahoolish, four internal jacks were activated to raise the load so that these baulks could be removed. The jacks were then lowered dropping the steel girders flat onto the bolsters so that the load could creep under two tight bridges yet still with an inch or two of clearance. The pots had a circuitous route to follow and watching them head north up the old A1 they resembled an old fashioned sailing clipper as they leaned over with the prevailing wind

5

On site — out of sight

Using crawlers to provide the propulsion as well as carrying the load does require a great deal of co-ordination amongst the machine operators. These Dennis Wompra photographs showing Rigging International's machines at work on the Laing's site at Graythorpe illustrate the type of object that they are quite able to transport. The CMP load is being moved in February 1974 by two 500 tonne capacity units whilst the 960 tonnes bottle leg section manufactured by Rheinstahl Noreseewerke for the BP Forties field has three 650 tonne capacity units underneath it during June of the same year. Close examination of the far right crawler of the three shows that the load support is allowed to float freely in what is termed as an ink well slider. This third machine does not provide any form of forward propulsion for the load but as the term suggests it allows movement in any direction of a great latitude thus making carriage that much easier. The wire ropes hanging down are the remains of fastenings used to secure the load on to the sea-going barge for its journey into the bay of Hartlepool

The mid-1970s was a busy time for heavy engineers Whessoe who are seen to be working hard on their Dock Point complex at Middlesbrough. Rigging International were also kept busy for at that time they were one of the few international companies that had both the equipment and the expertise to move objects that would take the breath away of even the recognized heavy hauliers of the day. The modular trailer concept hadn't really caught on in 1975 although bending this Forties Delta module around the obstructions in the yard really demonstrated the manoeuvrability of the two 500 tonne capacity and two 600 tonne capacity crawlers for at 1900 tonnes this module was exceptionally heavy for the era

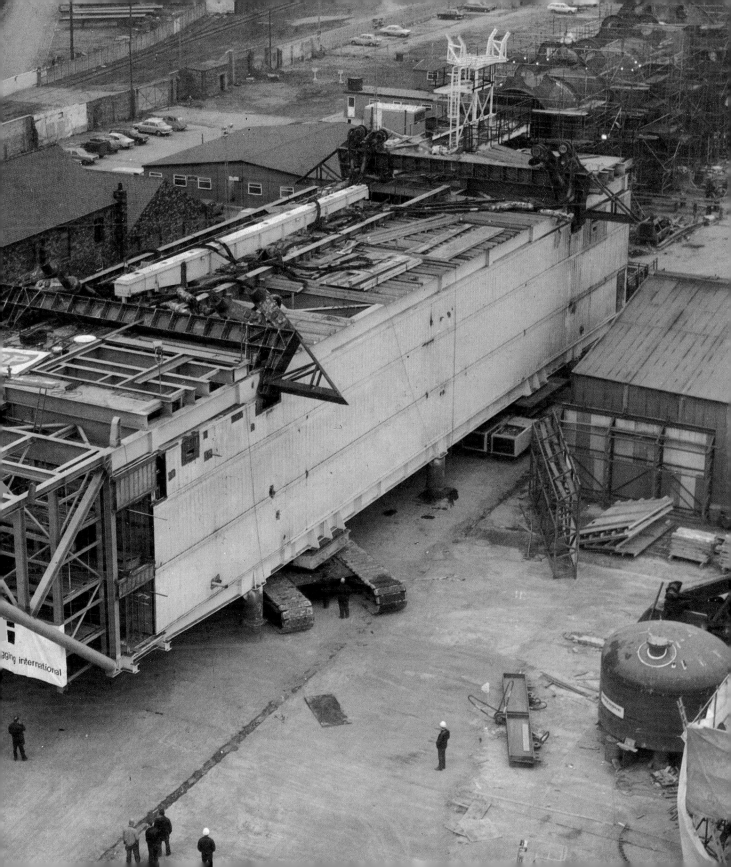

Some indication of the activity that goes on when a module is loaded out can be seen in this Whessoe photograph taken about 1978. Winches pulling the load are mounted midway down the barge with their wires going through pulleys at the extreme end. Operated like this it is possible to haul the module right down the 300 ft long barge thus leaving space for another similar load. Ballasted tractors TRL 924H and NPY 439P which seem well anchored down are having an easy time of it for their winches are simply being released and thus allowing the load to go away from them. They are of course being held in immediate readiness should it be necessary to reverse the direction of the module and quickly winch it back onto the quay

Sunters weren't the only operators to haul prefabricated units into Sullom Voe oil terminal for Rigging International hauled more than their fair share. Riggings similarly used modular trailers although their locomotion was entirely different to the North Yorkshire haulier's Scammells and Titans. Seen in shot hauling an HCG module which has been ro-ro'd from Holland is Rigging's faithful Hough. To all who saw it work, the 4×4 machine had more than enough power although on occasion Rigging were known to double head using one of their Lampson crawlers. One slight idiosyncrasy of the Hough because of its inbuilt articulation was that it was known to snap trailer drawbars if the driver tried to cut a corner too quickly. The machine had a 450 bhp Detroit engine with an Allison automatic gearbox. Its 67 tonne kerb weight was created by filling the balloon tyres with ballasting powder. The Hough was in fact a Vietnam veteran being bought from the American Army by a Dutchman and thence on to Rigging

Right As well as being near neighbours geographically, J. D. Whites of Thornaby and Sunters of Northallerton are both sister companies of the massive British Electric Traction Group. Grayston-White, as they are now known, are one of the big crane operators in the UK in both senses of the word and on show is their plant number 103501 Demag TC2000 lifting 115 tonnes of prefabricated rack at the maker's yard on Tyneside. The crane is fitted with a 137 ft 10 in. long boom and superlift backmast to give 400 tonnes lifting capacity. Tommy Doyle is at the controls of the machine, the yellow blocks littered about the crane being in total 236 tonnes of counterweight to allow this feat to be performed. The lift is done through a specially constructed lifting frame so the new rack can remain distortion free

Below A typical scene of one of the Tyneside construction yards in the late 1970s shows two of Sunters' ballasted tractors about to push their impressive Nicolas trailers underneath the closely adjacent module. Those on the left being older 12 ft wide heavyweight whilst the line on the right is new 9 ft 8 in. wide lightweight versions of the French product. This wasn't to be loaded out but Contractors LAJ 798P and NAJ 103P simply moved the 1182 tonnes across the yard to allow the module to its right to be moved to the left which in turn then allowed the manufacturers to commence building on yet another module. Four of Rigging International's massive 500 tonne capacity crawlers are pictured immediately in front of shot

If you have ever tried to climb into a canoe sideways you will know the sort of instability that is created in such a manoeuvre. Loading out sideways on to a barge has similar difficulties but when Rigging International were asked if they could do this with two 400 tonne production modules destined for the Leman field to suit the offshore unloading requirements, they were more than able to perform. Sideways ballasting is a major problem although the two tractors seen in use at the Charlton Leslie yard on the River Tyne were both fitted with torque converters ensuring a very smooth move. Mick Crowshaw is at the wheel of N12 PBE 867S whilst the brand new F12 is WEE 512V. Extra long drawbars were used so discounting the possibility of either Volvo getting on to the *Norbarge II*

Below Quite a load by normal standards but at 600 tonnes this production module for Chevron required only one locomotive to move it round the site of Charlton Leslie of Tyneside prior to being loaded out by ITM-Sunter during 1979. Hauling 16 rows of Nicolas axles the tractor was not normal either, by any standard. Titan VVN 910S is no mean performer. Pictured at the wheel on this day is Ken Bickerton who has occupied this left-hand seat for nearly all the vehicle's life since it came to Northallerton in 1977. As the temporary ballast box suggests, the 6×4 machine was purchased primarily for articulated use but with the capability of hauling four figure's worth of payload, it is only natural that Sunters regularly use the Titan in this ballasted form. Directing operations are Brian Pearson and Charles Tomkins, the former being one of the original founders of ITM

Right Tony McPartland had to have a strong head for heights but for heavy haulage enthusiasts he recorded quite a memorable occasion when Rigging International managed the movement of this Whessoe module at Dock Point, Middlesbrough. TSL provided the firepower with PBE 867S and WEE 512V but at 2000 tonnes it was felt that assistance in the shape of Econofreight's UVN 44S and Watkinson's LFB 716K should be coupled up to help. The differing new and not so new types of transmission weren't really conducive to smooth progress so once the inertia was broken, the Contractors were unhooked. The load was supported on four, 20-row trailers which at the time was the longest which could negotiate the infamous Whessoe ramp but for all on site it was still a nail-biting day

In March 1983 Mammoet-Econofreight provided a complete handling package for the delivery of a 335 tonne, 116 ft long, 36 ft wide floatation tank from Head Wrightson at Middlesbrough to McDermott's fabrication yard at Ardersier. They were first asked to jack the tank up to a height of 12 ft to allow Head to complete underside fabrication work. The load was then jacked down on to two independent hydraulic trailers and moved out to the quayside. Drivers Ernie Pickersgill and Alan Gilyeat are seen sitting underneath Middlesbrough's Transporter Bridge awaiting its ship whilst the umbilical cord joining the trailers ensured that the trailerman could brake both the load carriers at the same time

Right Commencing in September 1982, Whessoe of Darlington manufactured four of these massive gas baffles, two of which were moved into Heysham II power station by ITM-Sunter. Inching the mass from the delivering barge ITM 2 in Heysham harbour was down to slow pulling winches, but once on the slipway four tractors were used to haul the load up the gradient. Once at the top of the ramp the baffle, whose skirt conceals 105 tonnes of supporting steelwork, had to be manoeuvred into exactly the right position, so that work including intricate weighing could be conducted upon it. This meticulous manoeuvring of well in excess of 1000 tonnes found two tractors at either end taking turns at pulling so that the 336-wheeled Nicolas load carrier could be placed exactly on the spot

Below In late 1983 Econofreight moved this 190 tonne gas oil separation skid 500 yards from its construction shop to underneath the gantry cranes of the Mammoet heavy lift ship *Happy Mammoth*. Underneath this skid is an eight-bed six Nicolas trailer but for the empty run between Middlesbrough and Southampton, the outfit ran as a 14-row trailer with the bed being carried on the top. The four-man crew rigged the trailer by simply using the inbuilt hydraulics to place the bed into position. The skid built by the Plenty Group Ltd and destined for Abu Dhabi was moved about by MGE 180V, a ballasted 6×4 Volvo F12, all up weight being close to 300 tonnes

Below During June of 1982 Mammoet-Econofreight loaded out this 2165 tonne module from the Linthorpe Dinsdale site of Redpath, Dorman & Long in Middlesbrough. Scammell Contractor TRL 924H *Betsy* is shepherding the mass towards the water's edge prepared to apply her brakes as and when required. The two massive winch ropes in the foreground are ran out but would be put into action should the load have to be pulled back for any reason. There are four separate trailers under the module at this time each having 24 rows with the line in camera being of Scheuerle manufacture

Right The ideal way a heavy haulage man likes to carry an offshore crane like this is to get the jib straight upwards. The fact that the top of the load may be 195 ft off the ground is not of so great a concern but with the crane in that position it means the centre of gravity should fall within the confines of the supporting frame, thus the carriage is more predictable. At 275 tonnes this Stothert and Pitt lifting mechanism is seen having just been pushed back on to a waiting barge during March 1984 *en route* to a British Gas rig in Morecambe Bay. Smooth control across Charlton Leslie's offshore yard at Wallsend was assured from the turbocharged Volvos at the hands of drivers Pickersgill and Angles for both these 6×4s are fitted with torque converters in their transmissions

Norwell Offshore at Great Yarmouth is the scene of this shot as Econofreight move a combined accommodation module and helideck which weighed in at approximately 650 tonnes. The pulling winch ropes are seen to be in a state of tension whilst the slack ropes on the far right of the shot are used for either braking or retrieval should circumstances dictate. It should be noted that the winches are pulling the load rather than the trailers and how level the situation is even with the quayside being a peculiar stepped type of construction. The odd lumps of steel lying about on the barge at front left of shot are the fastenings that support the load when the trailers are removed

Moving an integrated deck like this naturally is far more difficult than moving a traditional type of module. Before anything like this can be moved, the haulier normally has to weigh the item meticulously and then design supporting steelwork to spread the weight across his trailers. This one loaded out of Norwell Offshore during the period 19–22 February 1984 was destined for Block 49/27-AQ in the North Sea. The rigs hauled out to the North Sea are widely different in construction with those destined for the Forties field and are obviously more sturdily constructed than the gas rigs used round the shallow waters off East Anglia. Both types benefit from the smooth support of the hydraulic suspension trailer which is shown to be working well in this shot taken by Tom Llewellyn

Prior to registration bonneted-142E CEE 464X took pride of place on the Scania stand in the 1982 Motor Show. Its immaculate paint job hasn't been touched apart from the occasional sticker adornment and only the privileged few know that its original owners were the Lincolnshire operators of Glazepen. It was regularly worked by G. E. Curtis (Heavy Haulage) Ltd and in 1983 they took over its ownership. Staying at the wheel for most of the tractor's life was Mick Crowshaw and one of the many loads moved by the Scania was this massive oil rig deck section. This was one of four similiar loads built by Haverton Hill Fabrications for UIE at Glasgow. Not the sort of load that is suitable to move up the A74, the 142E hauled the 400 tonne mass out the shop and loaded it on to a barge for the sea journey to Scotland

Left With production modules getting larger and more complex, even greater numbers of hydraulic axles get utilized and in moving this production module destined for Mobil's Beryl B field at Port Clarence, ITM-Sunter claimed that the 1120-wheeled load carrier was the largest trailer to be assembled. Just as the Sunter's locomotives are there should an emergency retrieval be required, the floating tug is seen in the shot to ensure the barge remains in position should anything untoward occur to the mooring winches. It may be thought that load outs are made simple with the use of these modular trailers but as the supporting lattice framework suggests, project engineers like Malcolm Rutter have a great deal of theoretical planning and design work to do before the charge can be lifted safely and moved into position

Below The four-legged deck sections are certainly one of the most impressive sights moved in the construction yards there being 1973 tonnes in this D3 Morecambe Bay module constructed by Press Production Systems at their Howden yard, Willington Quay, Wallsend. ITM-Sunter utilized four four-file Nicolas trailers each with 14 axles for the move in January 1984 although they were paired up with tie beams to ensure rigidity which also acted as interconnecting drawbars. Having a sideways tolerance of only $\frac{3}{8}$th of an inch steering the trailers was particularly critical so when the rear right one got slightly out of line, the track rods were disconnected and chain blocks used to pull the little wheels round

Above There were 2000 tonnes in this module 05 destined for Marathon Oil's Brae field in the North Sea that is seen at Charlton Leslie's yard at Wallsend. The awkward width of the load dictated to ITM that it was more efficient to leave the module at this end of the sea going mount, then turn the barge round before loading the other half rather than winching it right to the far end. Two four-file trailers with interconnecting spacers were used to take the weight and operations manager Brian Pearson is seen to be checking on the alignment and suspension as the move is in its critical stage. Mounted on the top of the module is the deep-sea crane lifting frame, the four giant lugs being called padears

Right 3106 tonnes of module, resting on 41 tonnes of supporting steelwork, moved on 396 tonnes of trailers adds up to 3543 tonnes or what ITM claimed to be the heaviest single weight moved on wheels. The integrated deck section destined for Britoil's Beatrice B platform was built by Cleveland Redpath Offshore at their Port Clarence yard and was loaded out during August 1983. The module was a significant achievement for the Teesside offshore construction company for they were not without their critics who said that such a large structure could not be built, never mind moved. With the figure of 4000 tonnes plus being whispered to be moved in 1985 there seems no limit to what the heavy movers can shift

During February 1984 Econofreight were involved in a load out of a particularly different kind in the moving of this near 1100 tonne pontoon destined for Sea Link at Harwich. Butterley Engineering of Ripley, Derbyshire had the contract to manufacture this construction and their original plans were to road haul the pieces to Harwich then assemble it in location. Lack of space precluded this operation and the building eventually took place at Haverton Hill in Cleveland. On completion, Econofreight's DAF WJH 288T assisted in dragging the load down to the low water mark where the front of the load was dropped on to concrete stools. The foremost set of Nicolas trailers were then retrieved sideways and as the tide came in and floated the pontoon free the rear Nicolas load carriers were kept energized so their soaking did them minimal harm

Left The heavy engineering company of Whessoe have produced quite a lot of impressive loads at their Dock Point, Middlesbrough complex but even they had to admit that this 885 tonne flareboom was perhaps something special. Mike Brown of Northern Photographic Services risked life and limb by getting into a crane bucket so that he could capture this 195 ft high mammoth in its true perspective. Rigging International were responsible for the movement across the yard and on to the waiting barge and the load is pictured halfway through its journey at the top of the Whessoe ramp. It took 40 minutes to descend the 100 yards down this incline, the smooth control being in the hands of winch operators Stuart Longburn and Gordon Maine. George Curtis provided two ballasted tractors but their role was purely to put air into Sarens' trailers to release or activate the spring brake units

Right Operations manager for this job was Norman Reid who would have preferred that the Goldhoffer modular trailers were rigged together sideways to give better support. However, the practical limitations imposed by the dimensions of the barge meant the 15 rows of axles were joined up lengthways and spreader joists used on the three load carriers to ensure all the wheels took their fair share of weight. The move was done on 17 April 1984, a date which Rigging had no choice over for this day coincided with the highest range of tide on the River Tees for the month, meaning that ballasting of the barge was particularly tricky. The flareboom is seen to be safely on the barge although move superintendent Alf Waller still had to take it even further inboard.

With the tide table not the clock dictating when load outs are performed it means that the heavy mover is sometimes hard at work when the rest of us are tucked up in bed. There is 1800 tonnes in this M1 module destined for the Central Production Platform in the Morecambe Bay gas field being winched backwards by ITM at Redpath Engineering on the River Tees. The large letter 'S' stands for south and indicates to the deep-sea crane operator which way round the module has to go on to the basic oil rig jacket. With this module being excessively wide, the eight ballasting pumps had to be placed through holes into the interior of the barge rather than being mounted on the edge of the deck. Module M8 was to follow this one on to the barge a couple of days later and along with two stair towers meant the load carrying sea mount was fully utilized if somewhat cluttered

Contents

Living a Dairy-Free Life

For some, the eating of any dairy products causes much misery and discomfort. For one reason or another people can be allergic to some or all dairy foods, which can include milk, yogurt, cream, butter and most cheeses. In some cases babies are born with an intolerance to lactose (present in cows' milk), and unless diagnosed early this can have a very disruptive effect. Often as the baby becomes a toddler they outgrow this intolerance. However, there are those who either do not or, for some reason, develop an intolerance to dairy products at a later date. In many cases there seems to be no reason for this, although some food experts feel that this reaction is due to intensive methods of farming and the way that animals are reared.

It is not only those who suffer an allergic reaction when eating dairy products who follow a dairy-free diet. For some, especially those following a low-fat diet, it makes perfect sense. Dairy products are high in saturated fats, meaning high cholesterol and calorie levels. So for those following a healthy heart or weight loss program, or those who are strict vegetarians or vegans, a dairy-free diet can be very beneficial.

For those who suffer a severe reaction when eating dairy products, the most probable reason is to do with the digestive system. Those who are lactose-intolerant do not produce the necessary enzymes needed to break down the sugar (called lactose) found in dairy products and the body cannot therefore absorb it. This can cause some distressing symptoms, including nausea, cramps, bloating, gas and an upset stomach. There is currently no cure for an intolerance to lactose, but the condition can be controlled by avoiding dairy products. The recipes in this book will help you to do this.

Many respected scientists and food experts feel that these problems, which have undoubtedly increased over the last fifty years, can be traced back to intensive farming methods. After the Second World War, the government instructed farmers to farm intensively in order that the country could not only feed its population but also have more than was needed. The excess could then be exported and less produce would need to be imported, thus helping the balance of payments. This intensive farming meant that fields where cattle herds grazed were treated with pesticides and the animal themselves were injected with growth hormones. This ensured that the animals came to maturity earlier and the milk yield was vastly increased. Animals were also regularly injected against disease.

Slowly, as more and more problems have appeared within the food chain, a backlash has occurred. There is a growing demand for animals to be treated more humanely and reared organically. A few farmers had continued or have returned to this method of traditional farming, and now the movement for organic farming – where the cattle are not treated with hormones and do not graze on land that has been treated with pesticides

– is steadily increasing. In theory at least, this ensures that neither the meat nor the milk and all the products that are made from the milk are contaminated. It has long been thought that these artificial hormones and pesticides can seriously affect the digestive system and set up allergies or a dairy intolerance.

In the United Kingdom, most milk and milk products are treated before being consumed, normally by pasteurization. This is a heat treatment that destroys any toxins that may be present in the milk or its products, such as yogurt, cheese, butter and cream. Unfortunately it also destroys the vitamins – especially vitamin D – contained in the milk. So the result is that these vitamins are artificially replaced. Some other countries still regularly use unpasteurized or 'raw' milk, so if there is any tendency to digestive or stomach problems it is a good idea to check whether the milk and its products are pasteurized or not when abroad.

If you are following a dairy-free diet it is important that the calcium and vitamins that we derive from milk are replaced by including other foods that contain them in the diet. Tofu, fish, especially salmon, all green leafy vegetables, nuts, sesame seeds and fruits such as dates are all good sources of calcium.

These days there are many substitutes for dairy products. Soya, rice, oat, almond, sunflower and coconut milks and their products make excellent substitutes and are available in most health food shops. Butter can be replaced with spreads made from vegetable or olive oils, and dairy-free butter is also available from larger supermarkets. Dairy-free cheeses are slightly more hit-and-miss, but again are available from supermarkets, as are soya creams, yogurts and ice creams.

Rather than providing substitutes, this book has been specifically designed to be dairy-free. There are plenty of delicious recipes to inspire you to cook healthy, nutritious meals suitable for all the family. From Aromatic Duck Burgers on Potato Pancakes to a Coconut Fish Curry and Pad Thai Noodles with Mushrooms, there's something for everyone here, whether they are following a dairy-free diet or not.

Aromatic Duck Burgers on Potato Pancakes

Nutritional details

per 100 g

energy	162 kcals/677 kj
protein	15 g
carbohydrate	7 g
fat	8 g
fibre	0.2 g
sugar	0.5 g
sodium	0.4 g

Ingredients   Serves 4

700 g/1½ lb boneless duck breasts
2 tbsp hoisin sauce
1 garlic clove, peeled and finely chopped
4 spring onions, trimmed
    and finely chopped
2 tbsp Japanese soy sauce
½ tsp Chinese five spice powder
salt and freshly ground black pepper
freshly chopped coriander, to garnish
extra hoisin sauce, to serve

For the potato pancakes:
450 g/1 lb floury potatoes
1 small onion, peeled and grated
1 small egg, beaten
1 heaped tbsp plain flour

Step-by-step guide

1 Peel off the thick layer of fat from the duck breasts and cut into small pieces. Put the fat in a small dry saucepan and set over a low heat for 10–15 minutes, or until the fat runs clear and the crackling goes crisp; reserve.

2 Cut the duck meat into pieces and blend in a food processor until coarsely chopped. Spoon into a bowl and add the hoisin sauce, garlic, half the spring onions, soy sauce and Chinese five spice powder. Season to taste with salt and pepper and shape into four burgers. Cover and chill in the refrigerator for 1 hour.

3 To make the potato pancakes, grate the potatoes into a large bowl, squeeze out the water with your hands, then put on a clean tea towel and twist the ends to squeeze out any remaining water. Return the potato to the bowl, add the onion and egg and mix well. Add the flour and salt and pepper. Stir to blend.

4 Heat about 2 tablespoons of the clear duck fat in a large frying pan. Spoon the potato mixture into 2–4 pattie shapes and cook for 6 minutes, or until golden and crisp, turning once. Keep warm in the oven. Repeat with the remaining mixture, adding duck fat as needed.

5 Preheat the grill and line the grill rack with tinfoil. Brush the burgers with a little of the duck fat and grill for 6–8 minutes, or longer if wished, turning once. Arrange 1–2 potato pancakes on a plate and top with a burger. Spoon over a little hoisin sauce and garnish with the remaining spring onions and coriander.

✓ cows' milk-free   ✓ egg-free   ✓ gluten-free   ✓ wheat-free   ✓ nut-free   vegetarian   vegan   ✓ seafood-free

Barbecued Fish Kebabs

Nutritional details

per 100 g

energy	116 kcals/486 kj
protein	9 g
carbohydrate	9 g
fat	5 g
fibre	0.3 g
sugar	7.4 g
sodium	0.3 g

Ingredients   Serves 4

450 g/1 lb herring or mackerel fillets,
   cut into chunks
2 small red onions, quartered
16 cherry tomatoes
 salt and freshly ground black pepper
freshly cooked couscous, to serve

For the sauce:
150 ml/¼ pint fish stock
5 tbsp tomato ketchup
2 tbsp Worcestershire sauce
2 tbsp wine vinegar
2 tbsp brown sugar
2 drops Tabasco
2 tbsp tomato purée

Step-by-step guide

1   Line a grill rack with a single layer of tinfoil and preheat the grill at a high temperature, 2 minutes before use.

2   If using wooden skewers, soak in cold water for 30 minutes to prevent them from catching alight during cooking.

3   Meanwhile, prepare the sauce. Add the fish stock, tomato ketchup, Worcestershire sauce, vinegar, sugar, Tabasco and tomato purée to a small saucepan. Stir well and leave to simmer for 5 minutes.

4   When ready to cook, drain the skewers, if necessary, then thread the fish chunks, the quartered red onions and the cherry tomatoes alternately on to the skewers.

5   Season the kebabs to taste with salt and pepper and brush with the sauce. Grill under the preheated grill for 8–10 minutes, basting with the sauce occasionally during cooking. Turn the kebabs often to ensure that they are cooked thoroughly and evenly on all sides. Serve immediately with couscous.

cows' milk-free   egg-free   gluten-free   wheat-free   nut-free   vegetarian   vegan   seafood-free   7

Battered Cod & Chunky Chips

Nutritional details

per 100 g

energy	210 kcals/883 kj
protein	9 g
carbohydrate	24 g
fat	9 g
fibre	1.3 g
sugar	0.4 g
sodium	0.1 g

Ingredients　　Serves 4

15 g/½ oz fresh yeast
300 ml/½ pint beer
225 g/8 oz plain flour
1 tsp salt
700 g/1½ lb potatoes
450 ml/¾ pint sunflower oil
4 cod fillets, about 225 g/8 oz each,
　　skinned and boned
2 tbsp seasoned plain flour

To garnish:
lemon wedges
sprigs of flat leaf parsley

To serve:
tomato ketchup
vinegar

Step-by-step guide

1　Dissolve the yeast with a little of the beer in a jug and mix to a paste. Pour in the remaining beer, whisking all the time until smooth. Place the flour and salt in a bowl, and gradually pour in the beer mixture, whisking continuously to make a thick, smooth batter. Cover the bowl and allow the batter to stand at room temperature for 1 hour.

2　Peel the potatoes and cut into thick slices. Cut each slice lengthways to make chunky chips. Place them in a non-stick frying pan and heat, shaking the pan until all the moisture has evaporated. Turn them onto absorbent kitchen paper to dry off.

3　Heat the oil to 180°C/350°F, then fry the chips a few at a time for 4–5 minutes until crisp and golden. Drain on absorbent kitchen paper and keep warm.

4　Pat the cod fillets dry, then coat in the flour. Dip the floured fillets into the reserved batter. Fry for 2–3 minutes until cooked and crisp, then drain. Garnish with lemon wedges and parsley and serve immediately with the chips, tomato ketchup and vinegar.

✓ cows' milk-free　✓ egg-free　✓ gluten-free　✓ wheat-free　✓ nut-free　✓ vegetarian　✓ vegan　✓ seafood-free

Beef Teriyaki with Green & Black Rice

Nutritional details

per 100 g

energy	151 kcals/633 kj
protein	16 g
carbohydrate	9 g
fat	5 g
fibre	0.4 g
sugar	3.2 g
sodium	0.3 g

Ingredients   Serves 4

3 tbsp sake (Japanese rice wine)
3 tbsp dry sherry
3 tbsp dark soy sauce
1½ tbsp soft brown sugar
4 sirloin steaks, each weighing
 175 g/6 oz, trimmed
350 g/12 oz long-grain
 and wild rice
2.5 cm/1 inch piece fresh
 root ginger
225 g/8 oz mangetout
6 spring onions, trimmed
 and cut into fine strips

Step-by-step guide

1 In a small saucepan, gently heat the sake, dry sherry, dark soy sauce and sugar until the sugar has dissolved. Increase the heat and bring to the boil. Remove from the heat and leave until cold. Lightly wipe the steaks, place in a shallow dish and pour the sake mixture over. Cover loosely and leave to marinate in the refrigerator for at least 1 hour, spooning the marinade over the steaks occasionally.

2 Cook the rice with the piece of root ginger, according to the packet instructions. Drain well, then remove and discard the piece of ginger.

3 Slice the mangetout thinly lengthways into fine shreds. Plunge into a saucepan of boiling salted water, return the water to the boil and drain immediately.

Stir the drained mangetout and spring onions into the hot rice.

4 Meanwhile, heat a griddle pan until almost smoking. Remove the steaks from the marinade and cook on the hot grill pan for 3–4 minutes each side, depending on the thickness.

5 Place the remaining marinade in a saucepan and bring to the boil. Simmer rapidly for 2 minutes and remove from the heat. When the steaks are cooked to personal preference, leave to rest for 2–3 minutes, then slice thinly and serve with the rice and the hot marinade.

☑ cows' milk-free ☑ egg-free ☑ gluten-free ☑ wheat-free ☑ nut-free ☑ vegetarian ☑ vegan ☑ seafood-free

9

Braised Chicken in Beer

Nutritional details

per 100 g

energy	89 kcals/377 kj
protein	10 g
carbohydrate	8 g
fat	2 g
fibre	1.6 g
sugar	4.3 g
sodium	0.1 g

Ingredients Serves 4

4 chicken joints, skinned
125 g/4 oz pitted dried prunes
2 bay leaves
12 shallots
2 tsp olive oil
125 g/4 oz small button
    mushrooms, wiped
1 tsp soft dark brown sugar
½ tsp wholegrain mustard
2 tsp tomato purée
150 ml/¼ pint light ale
150 ml/¼ pint chicken stock
salt and freshly ground
    black pepper
2 tsp cornflour
2 tsp lemon juice
2 tbsp chopped fresh parsley
flat leaf parsley, to garnish

To serve:
mashed potatoes
seasonal green vegetables

Step-by-step guide

1 Preheat the oven to 170°C/ 325°F/Gas Mark 3. Cut each chicken joint in half and put in an ovenproof casserole with the prunes and bay leaves.

2 To peel the shallots, put in a small bowl and cover with boiling water.

3 Drain the shallots after 2 minutes and rinse under cold water until cool enough to handle. The skins should then peel away easily from the shallots.

4 Heat the oil in a large, non-stick frying pan. Add the shallots and gently cook for about 5 minutes until beginning to colour.

5 Add the mushrooms to the pan and cook for a further 3–4 minutes until both the mushrooms and onions are softened.

6 Sprinkle the sugar over the shallots and mushrooms, then add the mustard, tomato purée, ale and chicken stock. Season to taste with salt and pepper and bring to the boil, stirring to combine. Carefully pour over the chicken.

7 Cover the casserole and cook in the preheated oven for 1 hour. Blend the cornflour with the lemon juice and 1 tablespoon of cold water and stir into the chicken casserole.

8 Return the casserole to the oven for a further 10 minutes or until the chicken is cooked and the vegetables are tender.

9 Remove the bay leaves and stir in the chopped parsley. Garnish the chicken with the flat leaf parsley. Serve with the mashed potatoes and fresh green vegetables.

✓ cows' milk-free ✓ egg-free ✓ gluten-free ✓ wheat-free ✓ nut-free ✓ vegetarian ✓ vegan ✓ seafood-free

Calypso Rice with Curried Bananas

Nutritional details

per 100 g

energy	109 kcals/457 kj
protein	3 g
carbohydrate	17 g
fat	4 g
fibre	1 g
sugar	7.4 g
sodium	0.1 g

Ingredients   Serves 4

2 tbsp sunflower oil
1 medium onion, peeled
    and finely chopped
1 garlic clove, peeled and crushed
1 red chilli, deseeded
    and finely chopped
1 red pepper, deseeded
    and chopped
225 g/8 oz basmati rice
juice of 1 lime
350 ml/12 fl oz vegetable stock
200 g can black-eye beans,
    drained and rinsed
2 tbsp freshly chopped parsley
salt and freshly ground
    black pepper
sprigs of coriander,
    to garnish

For the curried bananas:
4 green bananas
2 tbsp sunflower oil
2 tsp mild curry paste
200 ml/7 fl oz coconut milk

Step-by-step guide

1   Heat the oil in a large frying pan and gently cook the onion for 10 minutes until soft. Add the garlic, chilli and red pepper and cook for 2–3 minutes.

2   Rinse the rice under cold running water, then add to the pan and stir. Pour in the lime juice and stock, bring to the boil, cover and simmer for 12–15 minutes, or until the rice is tender and the stock is absorbed.

3   Stir in the black-eye beans and chopped parsley and season to taste with salt and pepper. Leave to stand, covered, for 5 minutes before serving to allow the beans to warm through.

4   While the rice is cooking, make the curried green bananas.

Remove the skins from the bananas – they may need to be cut off with a sharp knife. Slice the flesh thickly. Heat the oil in a frying pan and cook the bananas, in two batches, for 2–3 minutes, or until lightly browned.

5   Pour the coconut milk into the pan and stir in the curry paste.

6   Add the banana slices to the coconut milk and simmer, uncovered, over a low heat for 8–10 minutes, or until the bananas are very soft and the coconut milk slightly reduced.

7   Spoon the rice onto warmed serving plates, garnish with coriander and serve immediately with the curried bananas.

✓ cows' milk-free ✓ egg-free ✓ gluten-free ✓ wheat-free ✓ nut-free ✓ vegetarian ✓ vegan ✓ seafood-free

Chicken & Baby Vegetable Stir Fry

Nutritional details

per 100 g

energy	63 kcals/263 kj
protein	6 g
carbohydrate	3 g
fat	3 g
fibre	1.5 g
sugar	2 g
sodium	0.2 g

Ingredients　　　Serves 4

2 tbsp groundnut oil

1 small red chilli,
　　deseeded and finely chopped

150 g/5 oz chicken breast
　　or thigh meat, skinned
　　and cut into cubes

2 baby leeks, trimmed and sliced

12 asparagus spears, halved

125 g/4 oz mangetout, trimmed

125 g/4 oz baby carrots,
　　trimmed and halved lengthways

125 g/4 oz fine green beans,
　　trimmed and diagonally sliced

125 g/4 oz baby sweetcorn,
　　diagonally halved

50 ml/2 fl oz chicken stock

2 tsp light soy sauce

1 tbsp dry sherry

1 tsp sesame oil

toasted sesame seeds,
　　to garnish

Step-by-step guide

1　Heat the wok until very hot and add the oil. Add the chopped chilli and chicken and stir-fry for 4–5 minutes, or until the chicken is cooked and golden.

2　Increase the heat, add the leeks to the chicken and stir-fry for 2 minutes. Add the asparagus spears, mangetout, baby carrots, green beans, and baby sweetcorn. Stir-fry for 3–4 minutes, or until the vegetables soften slightly but still retain a slight crispness.

3　In a small bowl, mix together the chicken stock, soy sauce, dry sherry and sesame oil. Pour into the wok, stir and cook until heated through. Sprinkle with the toasted sesame seeds and serve immediately.

　　✓ cows' milk-free　✓ egg-free　✓ gluten-free　✓ wheat-free　✓ nut-free　✓ vegetarian　✓ vegan　✓ seafood-free

Chicken Basquaise

Nutritional details

per 100 g

energy	157 kcals/660 kj
protein	18 g
carbohydrate	5 g
fat	7 g
fibre	0.5 g
sugar	1.4 g
sodium	0.3 g

Ingredients   Serves 4–6

1.4 kg/3 lb chicken,
    cut into 8 pieces
2 tbsp plain flour
salt and freshly ground
    black pepper
3 tbsp olive oil
1 large onion,
    peeled and sliced
2 red peppers, deseeded and
    cut into thick strips
2 garlic cloves,
    peeled and crushed
150 g/5 oz spicy chorizo sausage
    cut into 1 cm/½ inch pieces
200 g/7 oz long-grain white rice
450 ml/¾ pint chicken stock
1 tsp crushed dried chillies
½ tsp dried thyme
1 tbsp tomato purée
125 g/4 oz Spanish air-dried
    ham, diced
12 black olives
2 tbsp freshly chopped parsley

Step-by-step guide

1 Dry the chicken pieces well with absorbent kitchen paper. Put the flour in a polythene bag, season with salt and pepper and add the chicken pieces. Twist the bag to seal, then shake to coat the chicken pieces thoroughly.

2 Heat 2 tablespoons of the oil in a large, heavy-based saucepan over a medium-high heat. Add the chicken pieces and cook for about 15 minutes, turning on all sides until well browned. Using a slotted spoon, transfer to a plate.

3 Add the remaining olive oil to the saucepan, then add the onion and peppers. Reduce the heat to medium and cook, stirring frequently, until starting to colour and soften. Stir in the garlic and chorizo and continue to cook for a further 3 minutes. Add the rice and cook for about 2 minutes, stirring to coat with the oil, until the rice is translucent and golden.

4 Stir in the stock, crushed chillies, thyme, tomato purée and salt and pepper and bring to the boil. Return the chicken to the saucepan, pressing gently into the rice. Cover and cook over a very low heat for about 45 minutes until the chicken and rice are cooked and tender.

5 Gently stir in the ham, black olives and half the parsley. Cover and heat for a further 5 minutes. Sprinkle with the remaining parsley and serve immediately.

Chicken Cacciatore

Nutritional details

per 100 g

energy	100 kcals/418 kj
protein	11 g
carbohydrate	6 g
fat	3 g
fibre	0.4 g
sugar	1.4 g
sodium	0.2 g

Ingredients   Serves 4

4 chicken leg portions
1 tbsp olive oil
1 red onion, peeled and
    cut into very thin wedges
1 garlic clove, peeled
    and crushed
sprig of fresh thyme
sprig of fresh rosemary
150 ml/¼ pint dry white wine
200 ml/7 fl oz chicken stock
400 g can chopped tomatoes
40 g/1½ oz black
    olives, pitted
15 g/½ oz capers, drained
salt and freshly ground
    black pepper
freshly cooked fettuccine,
    linguine or pasta shells

Step-by-step guide

1 Skin the chicken portions and cut each one into 2pieces to make four thighs and four drumsticks.

2 Heat 2 teaspoons of the oil in a flameproof casserole dish and cook the chicken for 2–3 minutes on each side until lightly browned. Remove the chicken from the pan and reserve.

3 Add the remaining 1 teaspoon of oil to the juices in the pan.

4 Add the red onion and gently cook for 5 minutes, stirring occasionally.

5 Add the garlic and cook for a further 5 minutes until soft and beginning to brown. Return the chicken to the pan.

6 Add the herbs, then pour in the wine and let it bubble for 1–2 minutes.

7 Add the stock and tomatoes, cover and gently simmer for 15 minutes.

8 Stir in the olives and capers. Cook uncovered for a further 5 minutes or until the chicken is cooked and the sauce thickened. Remove the herbs and season to taste with salt and pepper.

9 Place the chicken on a bed of pasta, allowing one thigh and one drumstick per person. Spoon over the sauce and serve.

cows' milk-free   egg-free   gluten-free   wheat-free   nut-free   vegetarian   vegan   seafood-free

Chinese Chicken Soup

Nutritional details

per 100 g

energy	79 kcals/335 kj
protein	11 g
carbohydrate	5 g
fat	2 g
fibre	0.8 g
sugar	1.4 g
sodium	0.8 g

Ingredients   Serves 4

225 g/8 oz cooked chicken
1 tsp oil
6 spring onions, trimmed
    and diagonally sliced
1 red chilli, deseeded
    and finely chopped
1 garlic clove, peeled
    and crushed
2.5 cm/1 inch piece
    root ginger, peeled
    and finely grated
1 litre/1¾ pint chicken stock
150 g/5 oz medium
    egg noodles
1 carrot, peeled and cut
    into matchsticks
125 g/4 oz beansprouts
2 tbsp soy sauce
1 tbsp fish sauce
fresh coriander leaves,
    to garnish

Step-by-step guide

1 Remove any skin from the chicken. Place on a chopping board and use two forks to tear the chicken into fine shreds.

2 Heat the oil in a large saucepan and fry the spring onions and chilli for 1 minute.

3 Add the garlic and ginger and cook for another minute.

4 Stir in the chicken stock and gradually bring the mixture to the boil.

5 Break up the noodles a little and add to the boiling stock with the carrot.

6 Stir to mix, then reduce the heat to a simmer and cook for 3–4 minutes.

7 Add the shredded chicken, beansprouts, soy sauce and fish sauce and stir.

8 Cook for a further 2–3 minutes until piping hot. Ladle the soup into bowls and sprinkle with the coriander leaves. Serve immediately.

✓ cows' milk-free ✓ egg-free ✓ gluten-free ✓ wheat-free ✓ nut-free ✓ vegetarian ✓ vegan ✓ seafood-free   **15**

Chinese-style Fried Rice

Nutritional details

per 100 g

energy	142 kcals/594 kj
protein	13 g
carbohydrate	11 g
fat	5 g
fibre	0.2 g
sugar	1 g
sodium	0.6 g

Ingredients   Serves 4-6

2–3 tbsp vegetable oil
2 small onions, peeled and
    cut into wedges
2 garlic cloves, peeled and thinly sliced
2.5 cm/1 inch piece of fresh
    root ginger, peeled and
    cut into thin slivers
225 g/8 oz cooked chicken,
    thinly sliced
125 g/4 oz cooked ham,
    thinly sliced
350 g/12 oz cooked cold
    long-grain white rice
125 g/4 oz canned water
    chestnuts, sliced
225 g/8 oz cooked peeled
    prawns (optional)
3 large eggs
3 tsp sesame oil
salt and freshly ground black pepper
6 spring onions, trimmed and sliced
    into 1 cm/½ inch pieces
2 tbsp dark soy sauce
1 tbsp sweet chilli sauce

2 tbsp freshly chopped coriander

To garnish:
2 tbsp chopped roasted peanuts
sprig of fresh coriander

Step-by-step guide

1 Heat a wok or large deep frying pan until very hot, add the oil and heat for 30 seconds. Add the onions and stir-fry for 2 minutes. Stir in the garlic and ginger and cook for 1 minute. Add the cooked sliced chicken and ham and stir-fry for a further 2–3 minutes.

2 Add the rice, the water chestnuts and prawns, if using, with 2 tablespoons of water, and stir-fry for 2 minutes until the rice is heated through.

3 Beat the eggs with 1 teaspoon of the sesame oil and season to taste with salt and pepper. Make a well in the centre of the rice, then pour in the egg mixture and stir immediately, gradually drawing the rice mixture into the egg, until the egg is cooked.

4 Add the spring onions, soy and chilli sauces, coriander and a little water, if necessary. Adjust the seasoning and drizzle with the remaining sesame oil. Sprinkle with the nuts and serve.

16   ✓ cows' milk-free   ✓ egg-free   ✓ gluten-free   ✓ wheat-free   ✓ nut-free   ✓ vegetarian   ✓ vegan   ✓ seafood-free

Coconut Fish Curry

Nutritional details

per 100 g

energy	139 kcals/583 kj
protein	9 g
carbohydrate	19 g
fat	3 g
fibre	0.4 g
sugar	2.6 g
sodium	0.2 g

Ingredients   Serves 4

2 tbsp sunflower oil
1 medium onion, peeled
    and very finely chopped
1 yellow pepper, deseeded
    and finely chopped
1 garlic clove, peeled and crushed
1 tbsp mild curry paste
2.5 cm/1 inch piece of root ginger,
    peeled and grated
1 red chilli, deseeded
    and finely chopped
400 ml can coconut milk
700 g/1½ lb firm white fish, e.g.
    monkfish fillets, skinned and
    cut into chunks
225 g/8 oz basmati rice
1 tbsp freshly chopped coriander
1 tbsp mango chutney
salt and freshly ground black pepper

To serve:
lime wedges
fresh coriander sprigs
Greek yogurt made from ewe's milk
warm naan bread

Step-by-step guide

1   Put 1 tablespoon of the oil into a large frying pan and cook the onion, pepper and garlic for 5 minutes, or until soft. Add the remaining oil, curry paste, ginger and chilli and cook for a further minute.

2   Pour in the coconut milk and bring to the boil, reduce the heat and simmer gently for 5 minutes, stirring occasionally. Add the monkfish to the pan and continue to simmer gently for 5–10 minutes, or until the fish is tender, but not overcooked.

3   Meanwhile, cook the rice in a saucepan of boiling salted water for 15 minutes, or until tender. Drain the rice thoroughly and turn out into a serving dish.

4   Stir the chopped coriander and chutney gently into the fish curry and season to taste with salt and pepper. Spoon the fish curry over the cooked rice, garnish with lime wedges and coriander sprigs and serve immediately with spoonfuls of Greek yogurt (avoid if intolerant of ewe's milk) and warm naan bread.

✔ cows' milk-free   ✔ egg-free   ✔ gluten-free   ✔ wheat-free   ✔ nut-free   ✔ vegetarian   ✔ vegan   ✔ seafood-free

Courgette & Tarragon Tortilla

Nutritional details

per 100 g

energy	118 kcals/496 kj
protein	4 g
carbohydrate	15 g
fat	5 g
fibre	1.3 g
sugar	1.5 g
sodium	trace

Ingredients   Serves 6

700 g/1½ lb potatoes
3 tbsp olive oil
1 onion, peeled
    and thinly sliced
salt and freshly ground
    black pepper
1 courgette, trimmed and
    thinly sliced
6 medium eggs
2 tbsp freshly chopped tarragon
tomato wedges, to serve

Step-by-step guide

1   Peel the potatoes and thinly slice. Dry the slices in a clean tea towel to get them as dry as possible. Heat the oil in a large heavy-based pan, add the onion and cook for 3 minutes. Add the potatoes with a little salt and pepper, then stir the potatoes and onion lightly to coat in the oil.

2   Reduce the heat to the lowest possible setting, cover and cook gently for 5 minutes. Turn the potatoes and onion over and continue to cook for a further 5 minutes. Give the pan a shake every now and again to ensure that the potatoes do not stick to the base or burn. Add the courgette, then cover and cook for a further 10 minutes.

3   Beat the eggs and tarragon together and season to taste with salt and pepper. Pour the egg mixture over the vegetables and return to the heat. Cook on a low heat for up to 20–25 minutes, or until there is no liquid egg left on the surface of the tortilla.

4   Turn the tortilla over by inverting it onto the lid or onto a flat plate. Return the pan to the heat and cook for a final 3–5 minutes, or until the underside is golden brown. If preferred, place the tortilla under a preheated grill for 4 minutes, or until set and golden brown on top. Cut into small squares and serve hot or cold with tomato wedges.

✓ cows' milk-free   ✓ egg-free   ✓ gluten-free   ✓ wheat-free   ✓ nut-free   ✓ vegetarian   ✓ vegan   ✓ seafood-free

Fried Ginger Rice with Soy Glazed Duck

Nutritional details

per 100 g

energy	158 kcals/660 kj
protein	10 g
carbohydrate	12 g
fat	8 g
fibre	0.5 g
sugar	4.8 g
sodium	0.6 g

Ingredients   Serves 4–6

2 duck breasts, skinned and
    diagonally cut into thin slices
2–3 tbsp Japanese soy sauce
1 tbsp mirin (sweet rice wine)
    or sherry
2 tbsp brown sugar
5 cm/2 inch piece of fresh
    root ginger, peeled and
    finely chopped
4 tbsp vegetable oil
2 garlic cloves, peeled and crushed
300 g/11 oz long-grain brown rice
900 ml/1½ pints chicken stock
freshly ground black pepper
125 g/4 oz lean ham, diced
175 g/6 oz mangetout,
    diagonally cut in half
8 spring onions, trimmed and
    diagonally thinly sliced
1 tbsp freshly chopped coriander
sweet or hot chilli sauce,
    to taste (optional)
sprigs of fresh coriander,
    to garnish

Step-by-step guide

1 Put the duck slices in a bowl with 1 tablespoon of the soy sauce, the mirin, 1 teaspoon of the sugar and one-third of the ginger; stir. Leave to stand.

2 Heat 2 tablespoons of the oil in a large, heavy-based saucepan. Add the garlic and half the remaining ginger and stir-fry for 1 minute. Add the rice and cook for 3 minutes, stirring constantly, until translucent.

3 Stir in all but 125 ml/4 fl oz of the stock, with 1 teaspoon of the soy sauce, and bring to the boil. Season with pepper. Reduce the heat to very low and simmer, covered, for 25–30 minutes until the rice is tender and the liquid is absorbed. Cover and leave to stand.

4 Heat the remaining oil in a large frying pan or wok. Drain the duck strips and add to the frying pan. Stir-fry for 2–3 minutes until just coloured. Add 1 tablespoon of soy sauce and the remaining sugar and cook for 1 minute until glazed. Transfer to a plate and keep warm.

5 Stir in the ham, mangetout, spring onions, the remaining ginger and the chopped coriander. Add the remaining stock and duck marinade and cook until the liquid is almost reduced. Fork in the rice and a little chilli sauce to taste, if using, and stir well. Turn into a serving dish and top with the duck. Garnish with coriander sprigs and serve immediately.

✓ cows' milk-free   ✓ egg-free   ✓ gluten-free   ✓ wheat-free   ✓ nut-free   ✓ vegetarian   ✓ vegan   ✓ seafood-free

Fruits de Mer Stir Fry

Nutritional details

per 100 g

energy	87 kcals/367 kj
protein	7 g
carbohydrate	10 g
fat	2 g
fibre	0.7 g
sugar	1 g
sodium	0.6 g

Ingredients   Serves 4

450 g/1 lb mixed fresh shellfish,
    such as tiger prawns, squid,
    scallops and mussels
2.5 cm/1 inch piece fresh root ginger
2 garlic cloves, peeled and crushed
2 green chillies, deseeded and
    finely chopped
3 tbsp light soy sauce
2 tbsp olive oil
200 g/7 oz baby sweetcorn, rinsed
200 g/7 oz asparagus tips,
    trimmed and cut in half
200 g/7 oz mangetout, trimmed
2 tbsp plum sauce
4 spring onions, trimmed
    and shredded, to garnish
freshly cooked rice, to serve

Step-by-step guide

1 Prepare the shellfish. Peel the
    prawns and, if necessary, remove
    the thin black veins from their
    backs. Lightly rinse the squid
    rings and clean the scallops
    if necessary.

2 Remove and discard any mussels
    that are open. Scrub and de-beard
    the remaining mussels, removing
    any barnacles from the shells.
    Cover the mussels with cold water
    until required.

3 Peel the root ginger and either
    coarsely grate or shred finely with
    a sharp knife and place into a
    small bowl.

4 Add the garlic and chillies to the
    small bowl, pour in the soy sauce
    and mix well.

5 Place the mixed shellfish, except
    the mussels, in a bowl and pour
    over the marinade. Stir, cover and
    leave for 15 minutes.

6 Heat a wok until hot, then add the
    oil and heat until almost smoking.
    Add the prepared vegetables, stir-
    fry for 3 minutes, then stir in the
    plum sauce.

7 Add the shellfish and the mussels
    with the marinade and stir-fry for
    a further 3–4 minutes, or until
    the fish is cooked. Discard any
    mussels that have not opened.
    Garnish with the spring onions
    and serve immediately with the
    freshly cooked rice.

cows' milk-free   egg-free   gluten-free   wheat-free   nut-free   vegetarian   vegan   seafood-free

Haddock with an Olive Crust

Nutritional details

per 100 g

energy	93 kcals/394 kj
protein	13 g
carbohydrate	6 g
fat	2 g
fibre	1.2 g
sugar	1.1 g
sodium	0.2 g

Ingredients   Serves 4

12 pitted black olives,
    finely chopped
75 g/3 oz fresh white
    breadcrumbs
1 tbsp freshly
    chopped tarragon
1 garlic clove,
    peeled and crushed
3 spring onions,
    trimmed and
    finely chopped
1 tbsp olive oil
4 x 175 g/6 oz thick skinless
    haddock fillets

To serve:
freshly cooked carrots
freshly cooked beans

Step-by-step guide

1 Preheat the oven to 190°C/ 375°F/Gas Mark 5. Place the black olives in a small bowl with the breadcrumbs and add the chopped tarragon.

2 Add the garlic to the olives with the chopped spring onions and the olive oil. Mix together lightly.

3 Wipe the fillets with either a clean damp cloth or damp kitchen paper, then place on a lightly oiled baking sheet.

4 Place spoonfuls of the olive and breadcrumb mixture on top of each fillet and press the mixture down lightly and evenly over the top of the fish.

5 Bake the fish in the preheated oven for 20–25 minutes or until the fish is cooked thoroughly and the topping is golden brown. Serve immediately with the freshly cooked carrots and beans.

Hoisin Chicken Pancakes

Nutritional details

per 100 g

energy	184 kcals/780 kj
protein	21 g
carbohydrate	21 g
fat	2 g
fibre	0.8 g
sugar	0.7 g
sodium	0.4 g

Ingredients   Serves 4

3 tbsp hoisin sauce
1 garlic clove,
    peeled and crushed
2.5 cm/1 inch piece root ginger,
    peeled and finely grated
1 tbsp soy sauce
1 tsp sesame oil
salt and freshly ground
    black pepper
4 skinless chicken thighs
½ cucumber, peeled
    (optional)
12 bought Chinese pancakes
6 spring onions, trimmed
    and cut lengthways
    into fine shreds
sweet chilli dipping sauce,
    to serve

Step-by-step guide

1 Preheat the oven to 190°C/
375°F/Gas Mark 5. In a non-
metallic bowl, mix the hoisin
sauce with the garlic, ginger, soy
sauce, sesame oil and seasoning.

2 Add the chicken thighs and turn to
coat in the mixture. Cover loosely
and leave in the refrigerator to
marinate for 3–4 hours, turning
the chicken from time to time.

3 Remove the chicken from
the marinade and place in a
roasting tin. Reserve the
marinade. Bake in the preheated
oven for 30 minutes, basting
occasionally with the marinade.

4 Cut the cucumber in half
lengthways and remove the seeds
by running a teaspoon down the
middle to scoop them out. Cut
into thin batons.

5 Place the pancakes in a steamer
to warm or heat according to
packet instructions. Thinly slice
the hot chicken and arrange on a
plate with the shredded spring
onions, cucumber and pancakes.

6 Place a spoonful of the chicken
in the middle of each warmed
pancake and top with pieces of
cucumber, spring onion, and a
little dipping sauce. Roll up and
serve immediately.

✓ cows' milk-free ✓ egg-free ✓ gluten-free ✓ wheat-free ✓ nut-free ✓ vegetarian ✓ vegan ✓ seafood-free

Honey & Ginger Prawns

Nutritional details

per 100 g

energy	71 kcals/300 kj
protein	10 g
carbohydrate	7 g
fat	0.6 g
fibre	0.7 g
sugar	6.7 g
sodium	0.8 g

Ingredients   Serves 4

1 carrot
50 g/2 oz bamboo shoots
4 spring onions
1 tbsp clear honey
1 tbsp tomato ketchup
1 tsp soy sauce
2.5 cm/1 inch piece fresh
    root ginger, peeled and
    finely grated
1 garlic clove,
    peeled and crushed
1 tbsp lime juice
175 g/6 oz peeled prawns,
    thawed if frozen
2 heads little gem lettuce leaves
2 tbsp freshly chopped coriander
salt and freshly ground
    black pepper

To garnish:
fresh coriander sprigs
lime slices

Step-by-step guide

1 Cut the carrot into matchstick-size pieces, roughly chop the bamboo shoots and finely slice the spring onions.

2 Combine the bamboo shoots with the carrot matchsticks and spring onions.

3 In a wok or large frying pan, gently heat the honey, tomato ketchup, soy sauce, ginger, garlic and lime juice with 3 tablespoons of water. Bring to the boil.

4 Add the carrot mixture and stir-fry for 2–3 minutes until the vegetables are hot.

5 Add the prawns and continue to stir-fry for 2 minutes.

6 Remove the wok or frying pan from the heat and reserve until cooled slightly.

7 Divide the little gem lettuce into leaves and rinse lightly.

8 Stir the chopped coriander into the prawn mixture and season to taste with salt and pepper. Spoon into the lettuce leaves and serve immediately garnished with sprigs of fresh coriander and lime slices.

cows' milk-free egg-free gluten-free wheat-free nut-free vegetarian vegan seafood-free

Huevos Rancheros

Nutritional details

per 100 g

energy	105 kcals/440 kj
protein	4 g
carbohydrate	13 g
fat	4 g
fibre	0.3 g
sugar	1.3 g
sodium	0.2 g

Ingredients   Serves 4

2 tbsp olive oil
1 large onion, peeled
    and finely chopped
1 red pepper, deseeded
    and finely chopped
2 garlic cloves, peeled
    and finely chopped
2–4 green chillies,
    deseeded and finely chopped
1 tsp ground cumin
1 tsp chilli powder
2 tsp ground coriander
2 tbsp freshly chopped coriander
700 g/1½ lb ripe plum
    tomatoes, peeled, deseeded
    and roughly chopped
¼ tsp sugar
8 small eggs
4–8 flour tortillas
salt and freshly ground
    black pepper
sprigs of fresh coriander,
    to garnish
refried beans, to serve
    (optional)

Step-by-step guide

1 Heat the oil in a large heavy-based saucepan. Add the onion and pepper and cook over a medium heat for 10 minutes.

2 Add the garlic, chillies, ground cumin, chilli powder and chopped coriander and cook for a further minute.

3 Add the tomatoes and sugar. Stir well, cover and cook gently for 20 minutes. Uncover and cook for a further 20 minutes.

4 Lightly poach the eggs in a large frying pan, filled with gently simmering water. Drain well and keep warm.

5 Place the tortillas briefly under a preheated hot grill. Turn once, then remove from the grill when crisp.

6 Add the freshly chopped coriander to the tomato sauce and season to taste with salt and pepper.

7 To serve, arrange two tortillas on each serving plate, top with two eggs and spoon the sauce over. Garnish with sprigs of fresh coriander and serve immediately with warmed refried beans, if liked.

24   ✓ cows' milk-free   ✓ egg-free   ✓ gluten-free   ✓ wheat-free   ✓ nut-free   ✓ vegetarian   ✓ vegan   ✓ seafood-free

Italian Bean Soup

Nutritional details

per 100 g

energy	97 kcals/406 kj
protein	5 g
carbohydrate	16 g
fat	2 g
fibre	0.7 g
sugar	0.6 g
sodium	0.3 g

Ingredients   Serves 4

2 tsp olive oil
1 leek, washed and chopped
1 garlic clove, peeled and crushed
2 tsp dried oregano
75 g/3 oz green beans,
    trimmed and cut into
    bite-size pieces
410 g can cannellini beans,
    drained and rinsed
75 g/3 oz small pasta shapes
1 litre/1¾ pint vegetable stock
8 cherry tomatoes
salt and freshly ground black pepper
3 tbsp freshly shredded basil

Step-by-step guide

1 Heat the oil in a large saucepan.
   Add the leek, garlic and oregano
   and cook gently for 5 minutes,
   stirring occasionally.

2 Stir in the green beans and the
   cannellini beans. Sprinkle in the
   pasta and pour in the stock.

3 Bring the stock mixture to the boil,
   then reduce the heat to a simmer.

4 Cook for 12–15 minutes or
   until the vegetables are tender
   and the pasta is 'al dente'.
   Stir occasionally.

5 In a heavy-based frying pan,
   dry-fry the tomatoes over a high
   heat until they soften and the
   skins begin to blacken.

6 Gently crush the tomatoes
   in the pan with the back of
   a spoon and add to the soup.

7 Season to taste with salt and
   pepper. Stir in the shredded basil
   and serve immediately.

✓ cows' milk-free ✓ egg-free ✓ gluten-free ✓ wheat-free ✓ nut-free ✓ vegetarian ✓ vegan ✓ seafood-free

25

Lamb Pilaf

Nutritional details

per 100 g

energy	130 kcals/542 kj
protein	8 g
carbohydrate	8 g
fat	7 g
fibre	0.8 g
sugar	1.8 g
sodium	0.1 g

Ingredients   Serves 4

2 tbsp vegetable oil
25 g/1 oz flaked or slivered almonds
1 medium onion,
    peeled and finely chopped
1 medium carrot,
    peeled and finely chopped
1 celery stalk,
    trimmed and finely chopped
350 g/12 oz lean lamb, cut into chunks
$\frac{1}{4}$ tsp ground cinnamon
$\frac{1}{4}$ tsp chilli flakes
2 large tomatoes, skinned,
    deseeded and chopped
grated rind of 1 orange
350 g/12 oz easy-cook brown
    basmati rice
600 ml/1 pint vegetable or lamb stock
2 tbsp freshly snipped chives
3 tbsp freshly chopped coriander
salt and freshly ground black pepper

To garnish:
lemon slices
sprigs of fresh coriander

Step-by-step guide

1 Preheat the oven to 140°C/
   275°F/Gas Mark 1. Heat the oil
   in a flameproof casserole dish
   with a tight-fitting lid and add the
   almonds. Cook for about 1 minute
   until just starting to brown,
   stirring often. Add the onion,
   carrot and celery and cook gently
   for a further 8–10 minutes until
   soft and lightly browned.

2 Increase the heat and add the lamb.
   Cook for a further 5 minutes until
   the lamb has changed colour. Add
   the ground cinnamon and chilli
   flakes and stir briefly before adding
   the tomatoes and orange rind.

3 Stir and add the rice, then the
   stock. Bring slowly to the boil and
   cover tightly. Transfer to the
   preheated oven and cook for
   30–35 minutes until the rice is
   tender and the stock is absorbed.

4 Remove from the oven and leave
   to stand for 5 minutes before
   stirring in the chives and
   coriander. Season to taste with
   salt and pepper. Garnish with the
   lemon slices and sprigs of fresh
   coriander and serve immediately.

✓ cows' milk-free   ✓ egg-free   ✓ gluten-free   ✓ wheat-free   ✓ nut-free   ✓ vegetarian   ✓ vegan   ✓ seafood-free

Marinated Vegetable Kebabs

Nutritional details

per 100 g

energy	56 kcals/236 kj
protein	2 g
carbohydrate	10 g
fat	1 g
fibre	0.2 g
sugar	0.5 g
sodium	0.2 g

Ingredients — Serves 4

2 small courgettes, cut into
2 cm/³⁄₄ inch pieces
½ green pepper, deseeded and
cut into 2.5 cm/1 inch pieces
½ red pepper, deseeded and cut
into 2.5 cm /1 inch pieces
½ yellow pepper, deseeded and
cut into 2.5 cm/1 inch pieces
8 baby onions, peeled
8 button mushrooms
8 cherry tomatoes
freshly chopped parsley, to garnish
freshly cooked couscous, to serve

For the marinade:
1 tbsp light olive oil
4 tbsp dry sherry
2 tbsp light soy sauce
1 red chilli, deseeded
and finely chopped
2 garlic cloves, peeled
and crushed
2.5 cm/1 inch piece root ginger,
peeled and finely grated

Step-by-step guide

1 Place the courgettes, peppers and baby onions in a pan of just-boiled water. Bring back to the boil and simmer for about 30 seconds.

2 Drain and rinse the cooked vegetables in cold water and dry on absorbent kitchen paper.

3 Thread the cooked vegetables and the mushrooms and tomatoes alternately on to skewers and place in a large, shallow dish.

4 Make the marinade by whisking all the ingredients together until thoroughly blended. Pour the marinade evenly over the kebabs, then chill in the refrigerator for at least 1 hour. Spoon the marinade over the kebabs occasionally during this time.

5 Place the kebabs in a hot griddle pan or on a hot barbecue and cook gently for 10–12 minutes. Turn the kebabs frequently and brush with the marinade when needed. When the vegetables are tender, sprinkle over the chopped parsley and serve immediately with couscous.

cows' milk-free · egg-free · gluten-free · wheat-free · nut-free · vegetarian · vegan · seafood-free

Mediterranean Feast

Nutritional details

per 100 g

energy	78 kcals/325 kj
protein	5 g
carbohydrate	5 g
fat	4 g
fibre	0.9 g
sugar	1.7 g
sodium	0.1 g

Ingredients   Serves 4

1 small iceberg lettuce
225 g/8 oz French beans
225 g/8 oz baby new
    potatoes, scrubbed
4 medium eggs
1 green pepper
1 medium onion, peeled
200 g can tuna in brine, drained
    and flaked into small pieces
8 ripe but firm cherry
    tomatoes, quartered
50 g/2 oz black pitted olives, halved
freshly chopped basil, to garnish

For the lime vinaigrette:

3 tbsp light olive oil
2 tbsp white wine vinegar
4 tbsp lime juice
grated rind of 1 lime
1 tsp gluten-free Dijon mustard
1-2 tsp caster sugar
salt and freshly ground
    black pepper

Step-by-step guide

1 Cut the lettuce into four and remove the hard core. Tear into bite-sized pieces and arrange on a large serving platter or four individual plates.

2 Cook the French beans in boiling salted water for 8 minutes and the potatoes for 10 minutes or until tender. Drain and rinse in cold water until cool, then cut both the beans and potatoes in half with a sharp knife.

3 Boil the eggs for 10 minutes, then rinse thoroughly under a cold running tap until cool. Remove the shells under water and cut each egg into four.

4 Remove the seeds from the pepper and cut into thin strips and finely chop the onion.

5 Arrange the beans, potatoes, eggs, peppers and onion on top of the lettuce. Add the tuna and tomatoes. Sprinkle over the olives and garnish with the basil.

6 To make the vinaigrette, place all the ingredients in a screw-topped jar and shake vigorously until everything is mixed thoroughly. Spoon 4 tablespoons over the top of the prepared salad and serve the remainder separately.

cows' milk-free   ✓ egg-free   ✓ gluten-free   ✓ wheat-free   ✓ nut-free   ✓ vegetarian   ✓ vegan   seafood-free

Oriental Minced Chicken on Rocket & Tomato

Nutritional details

per 100 g

energy	105 kcals/442 kj
protein	15 g
carbohydrate	4 g
fat	3 g
fibre	0.4 g
sugar	1.1 g
sodium	0.3 g

Ingredients   Serves 4

2 shallots, peeled
1 garlic clove, peeled
1 carrot, peeled
50 g/2 oz water chestnuts
1 tsp oil
350 g/12 oz fresh
    chicken mince
1 tsp Chinese five spice powder
pinch chilli powder
1 tsp soy sauce
1 tbsp fish sauce
8 cherry tomatoes
50 g/2 oz rocket

Step-by-step guide

1   Finely chop the shallots and garlic. Cut the carrot into matchsticks, thinly slice the water chestnuts and reserve. Heat the oil in a wok or large, heavy-based frying pan and add the chicken. Stir-fry for 3–4 minutes over a moderately high heat, breaking up any large pieces of chicken.

2   Add the garlic and shallots and cook for 2–3 minutes until softened. Sprinkle over the Chinese five spice powder and the chilli powder and continue to cook for about 1 minute.

3   Add the carrot, water chestnuts, soy and fish sauce and 2 tablespoons of water. Stir-fry for a further 2 minutes. Remove from the heat and reserve to cool slightly.

4   Deseed the tomatoes and cut into thin wedges. Toss with the rocket and divide between four serving plates. Spoon the warm chicken mixture over the rocket and tomato wedges and serve immediately to prevent the rocket from wilting.

cows' milk-free   egg-free   gluten-free   wheat-free   nut-free   vegetarian   vegan   seafood-free   29

Pad Thai Noodles with Mushrooms

Nutritional details

per 100 g

energy	122 kcals/507 kj
protein	4 g
carbohydrate	11 g
fat	7 g
fibre	0.6 g
sugar	1.2 g
sodium	0.4 g

Ingredients   Serves 4

125 g/4 oz flat rice noodles
   or rice vermicelli
1 tbsp vegetable oil
2 garlic cloves,
   peeled and finely chopped
1 medium egg, lightly beaten
225 g/8 oz mixed mushrooms,
   including shiitake, oyster, field,
   brown and wild mushrooms
2 tbsp lemon juice
1½ tbsp Thai fish sauce
½ tsp sugar
½ tsp cayenne pepper
2 spring onions,
   trimmed and cut into
   2.5 cm/1 inch pieces
50 g/2 oz fresh beansprouts

To garnish:
chopped roasted peanuts
freshly chopped coriander

Step-by-step guide

1   Cook the noodles according to the packet instructions. Drain well and reserve.

2   Heat a wok or large frying pan. Add the oil and garlic. Fry until just golden. Add the egg and stir quickly to break it up.

3   Cook for a few seconds before adding the noodles and mushrooms. Scrape down the sides of the pan to ensure they mix with the egg and garlic.

4   Add the lemon juice, fish sauce, sugar, cayenne pepper, spring onions and half of the beansprouts, stirring quickly all the time.

5   Cook over a high heat for a further 2–3 minutes until everything is heated through.

6   Turn on to a serving plate and top with the remaining beansprouts. Garnish with the chopped peanuts and coriander and serve immediately.

✓ cows' milk-free   ✓ egg-free   ✓ gluten-free   ✓ wheat-free   ✓ nut-free   ✓ vegetarian   ✓ vegan   ✓ seafood-free

Pan-cooked Chicken with Thai Spices

Nutritional details

per 100 g

energy	133 kcals/560 kj
protein	21 g
carbohydrate	8 g
fat	2 g
fibre	0.4 g
sugar	trace
sodium	0.3 g

Ingredients   Serves 4

4 kaffir lime leaves
5 cm/2 inch piece of root
    ginger, peeled and chopped
300 ml/½ pint chicken
    stock, boiling
4 x 175 g/6 oz chicken breasts
2 tsp groundnut oil
5 tbsp coconut milk
1 tbsp fish sauce
2 red chillies,
    deseeded and
    finely chopped
225 g/8 oz Thai jasmine rice
1 tbsp lime juice
3 tbsp freshly chopped coriander
salt and freshly ground
    black pepper

To garnish:
wedges of lime
freshly chopped coriander

Step-by-step guide

1. Lightly bruise the kaffir lime leaves and put in a bowl with the chopped ginger. Pour over the chicken stock, cover and leave to infuse for 30 minutes.

2. Meanwhile, cut each chicken breast into two pieces. Heat the oil in a large, non-stick frying pan or flameproof casserole dish and brown the chicken pieces for 2–3 minutes on each side.

3. Strain the infused chicken stock into the pan. Half cover the pan with a lid and gently simmer for 10 minutes.

4. Stir in the coconut milk, fish sauce and chopped chillies. Simmer, uncovered for 5–6 minutes, or until the chicken is tender and cooked through and the sauce has reduced slightly.

5. Meanwhile, cook the rice in boiling salted water according to the packet instructions. Drain the rice thoroughly.

6. Stir the lime juice and chopped coriander into the sauce. Season to taste with salt and pepper. Serve the chicken and sauce on a bed of rice. Garnish with wedges of lime and freshly chopped coriander and serve immediately.

✓ cows' milk-free   ✓ egg-free   ✓ gluten-free   ✓ wheat-free   ✓ nut-free   ✓ vegetarian   ✓ vegan   ✓ seafood-free

Pork Loin Stuffed with Orange & Hazelnut Rice

Nutritional details

per 100 g

energy	116 kcals/485 kj
protein	13 g
carbohydrate	4 g
fat	5 g
fibre	0.9 g
sugar	2.6 g
sodium	0.2 g

Ingredients   Serves 4

1 tbsp olive oil
1 shallot, peeled and
    finely chopped
50 g/2 oz long-grain brown rice
175 ml/6 fl oz vegetable stock
½ orange
25 g/1 oz ready-to-eat dried prunes,
    stoned and chopped
25 g/1 oz hazelnuts,
    roasted and roughly chopped
1 small egg, beaten
1 tbsp freshly chopped parsley
salt and freshly ground pepper
450 g/1 lb boneless pork
    tenderloin or fillet,
    trimmed

For the rice:
steamed courgettes
carrots

Step-by-step guide

1 Preheat the oven to 190°C/ 375°F/Gas Mark 5, 10 minutes before required. Heat the oil in a small saucepan, add the shallot and cook gently for 2–3 minutes until softened. Add the rice and stir well for 1 minute. Add the stock, stir well and bring to the boil. Cover tightly and simmer gently for 30 minutes until the rice is tender and all the liquid is absorbed. Leave to cool.

2 Grate the orange rind and reserve. Remove the white pith and chop the orange flesh finely. Mix together the orange rind and flesh, prunes, hazelnuts, cooled rice, egg and parsley. Season to taste with salt and pepper.

3 Cut the fillet in half, then using a sharp knife, split the pork fillet lengthways almost in two, forming a pocket, leaving it just attached. Open out the pork and put between two pieces of clingfilm. Flatten using a meat mallet until about half its original thickness. Spoon the filling into the pocket and close the fillet over. Tie along the length with kitchen string at regular intervals.

4 Put the pork fillet in a small roasting tray and cook in the top of the preheated oven for 25–30 minutes, or until the meat is just tender. Remove from the oven and allow to rest for 5 minutes. Slice into rounds and serve with steamed courgettes and carrots.

cows' milk-free ✓ egg-free ✓ gluten-free ✓ wheat-free ✓ nut-free ✓ vegetarian ✓ vegan ✓ seafood-free

Prawn & Chilli Soup

Nutritional details

per 100 g

energy	72 kcals/304 kj
protein	13 g
carbohydrate	4 g
fat	1 g
fibre	trace
sugar	0.5 g
sodium	1.2 g

Ingredients   Serves 4

2 spring onions, trimmed
225 g/8 oz whole raw tiger prawns
750 ml/1¼ pint fish stock
finely grated rind and juice
    of 1 lime
1 tbsp fish sauce
1 red chilli, deseeded and chopped
1 tbsp soy sauce
1 lemon grass stalk
2 tbsp rice vinegar
4 tbsp freshly chopped coriander

Step-by-step guide

1 To make spring onion curls, finely shred the spring onions lengthways. Place in a bowl of iced cold water and reserve.

2 Remove the heads and shells from the prawns leaving the tails intact.

3 Split the prawns almost in two to form a butterfly shape and individually remove the black thread that runs down the back of each one.

4 In a large pan heat the stock with the lime rind and juice, fish sauce, chilli and soy sauce.

5 Bruise the lemon grass by crushing it along its length with a rolling pin, then add to the stock mixture.

6 When the stock mixture is boiling add the prawns and cook until they are pink.

7 Remove the lemon grass and add the rice vinegar and coriander.

8 Ladle into bowls and garnish with the spring onion curls. Serve immediately.

☑ cows' milk-free ☑ egg-free ☑ gluten-free ☑ wheat-free ☑ nut-free ☑ vegetarian ☑ vegan ☑ seafood-free   33

Rice & Tomato Soup

Nutritional details

per 100 g

energy	132 kcals/555 kj
protein	3 g
carbohydrate	16 g
fat	7 g
fibre	0.7 g
sugar	2.5 g
sodium	0.3 g

Ingredients   Serves 4

150 g/5 oz easy-cook
   basmati rice
400 g can chopped tomatoes
2 garlic cloves,
   peeled and crushed
grated rind of ½ lime
2 tbsp extra virgin olive oil
1 tsp sugar
salt and freshly
   ground pepper
300 ml/½ pint vegetable
   stock or water

For the croûtons:
2 tbsp dairy-free pesto sauce
2 tbsp olive oil
6 thin slices ciabatta bread,
   cut into 1 cm/½ inch cubes

Step-by-step guide

1 Preheat the oven to 220°C/
   425°F/Gas Mark 7. Rinse and
   drain the basmati rice. Place the
   canned tomatoes with their juice
   in a large, heavy-based saucepan
   with the garlic, lime rind, oil and
   sugar. Season to taste with salt
   and pepper. Bring to the boil, then
   reduce the heat, cover and
   simmer for 10 minutes.

2 Add the boiling vegetable stock
   or water and the rice, then cook,
   uncovered, for a further 15–20
   minutes, or until the rice is tender.
   If the soup is too thick, add a
   little more water. Reserve and
   keep warm, if the croûtons are
   not ready.

3 Meanwhile, to make the croûtons,
   mix the pesto and olive oil in a
   large bowl. Add the bread cubes
   and toss until they are coated
   completely with the mixture.
   Spread on a baking sheet and
   bake in the preheated oven for
   10–15 minutes, until golden and
   crisp, turning them over halfway
   through cooking. Serve the soup
   immediately sprinkled with the
   warm croûtons.

cows' milk-free   egg-free   gluten-free   wheat-free   nut-free   vegetarian   vegan   seafood-free

Roasted Aubergine Dip with Pitta Strips

Nutritional details

per 100 g

energy	51 kcals/216 kj
protein	2 g
carbohydrate	11 g
fat	0.4 g
fibre	0.3 g
sugar	0.4 g
sodium	trace

Ingredients   Serves 4

4 pitta breads
2 large aubergines
1 garlic clove, peeled
¼ tsp sesame oil
1 tbsp lemon juice
½ tsp ground cumin
salt and freshly ground
    black pepper
2 tbsp freshly chopped parsley
fresh salad leaves,
    to serve

Step-by-step guide

1   Preheat the oven to 180°C/ 350°F/Gas Mark 4. On a chopping board cut the pitta breads into strips. Spread the bread in a single layer on to a large baking tray.

2   Cook in the preheated oven for 15 minutes until golden and crisp. Leave to cool on a wire cooling rack.

3   Trim the aubergines, rinse lightly and reserve. Heat a griddle pan until almost smoking. Cook the aubergines and garlic for about 15 minutes.

4   Turn the aubergines frequently, until very tender with wrinkled and charred skins. Remove from heat. Leave to cool.

5   When the aubergines are cool enough to handle, cut in half,

scoop out the cooked flesh and place in a food processor.

6   Squeeze the softened garlic flesh from the papery skin and add to the aubergine.

7   Blend the aubergine and garlic until smooth, then add the sesame oil, lemon juice and cumin and blend again to mix.

8   Season to taste with salt and pepper, stir in the parsley and serve with the pitta strips and mixed salad leaves.

cows' milk-free ✓ egg-free ✓ gluten-free ✓ wheat-free ✓ nut-free ✓ vegetarian ✓ vegan ✓ seafood-free

Roasted Red Pepper, Tomato & Red Onion Soup

Nutritional details

per 100 g

energy	65 kcals/278 kj
protein	2 g
carbohydrate	13 g
fat	0.7 g
fibre	1.7 g
sugar	4.9 g
sodium	0.3 g

Ingredients   Serves 4

fine spray of oil
2 large red peppers,
    deseeded and
    roughly chopped
1 red onion, peeled and
    roughly chopped
350 g/12 oz tomatoes, halved
1 small crusty French loaf
1 garlic clove, peeled
600 ml/1 pint vegetable stock
salt and freshly ground
    black pepper
1 tsp Worcestershire sauce

Step-by-step guide

1   Preheat the oven to 190°C/
    375°F/Gas Mark 5. Spray a large
    roasting tin with the oil and place
    the peppers and onion in the
    base. Cook in the oven for 10
    minutes. Add the tomatoes and
    cook for a further 20 minutes or
    until the peppers are soft.

2   Cut the bread into 1 cm/½ inch
    slices. Cut the garlic clove in half
    and rub the cut edge of the garlic
    over the bread.

3   Place all the bread slices on a
    large baking tray, and bake in the
    preheated oven for 10 minutes,
    turning halfway through, until
    golden and crisp.

4   Remove the vegetables from the
    oven and allow to cool slightly,
    then blend in a food processor
    until smooth. Strain the vegetable
    mixture through a large nylon
    sieve into a saucepan, to remove
    the seeds and skin. Add the stock,
    season to taste with salt and
    pepper and stir to mix. Heat the
    soup gently until piping hot.

5   In a small bowl beat together the
    Worcestershire sauce with the
    fromage frais.

6   Pour the soup into warmed
    bowls and serve immediately
    with the garlic toasts.

cows' milk-free   egg-free   gluten-free   wheat-free   nut-free   vegetarian   vegan   seafood-free

Royal Fried Rice

Nutritional details

per 100 g

energy	107 kcals/445 kj
protein	5 g
carbohydrate	13 g
fat	4 g
fibre	0.1 g
sugar	0.9 g
sodium	0.3 g

Ingredients   Serves 4

450 g/1 lb Thai fragrant rice
2 large eggs
2 tsp sesame oil
salt and freshly ground black pepper
3 tbsp vegetable oil
1 red pepper,
   deseeded and finely diced
1 yellow pepper,
   deseeded and finely diced
1 green pepper,
   deseeded and finely diced
2 red onions, peeled and diced
125 g/4 oz sweetcorn kernels
125 g/4 oz cooked peeled prawns,
   thawed if frozen
125 g/4 oz white crabmeat,
   drained if canned
$\frac{1}{4}$ tsp sugar
2 tsp light soy sauce

To garnish:
radish roses
freshly snipped and whole
   chive leaves

Step-by-step guide

1 Place the rice in a sieve, rinse with cold water, then drain. Place in a saucepan and add twice the volume of water, stirring briefly. Bring to the boil, cover and simmer gently for 15 minutes without further stirring. If the rice has fully absorbed the water while covered, add a little more water. Continue to simmer, uncovered, for another 5 minutes or until the rice is fully cooked and the water has evaporated. Leave to cool.

2 Place the eggs, sesame oil and a pinch of salt in a small bowl. Using a fork, mix just to break the egg. Reserve.

3 Heat a wok and add 1 tablespoon of the vegetable oil. When very hot, stir-fry the peppers, onion and sweetcorn for 2 minutes or until the onion is soft. Remove the vegetables and reserve.

4 Clean the wok and add the remaining oil. When very hot, add the cold cooked rice and stir-fry for 3 minutes, or until it is heated through. Drizzle in the egg mixture and continue to stir-fry for 2–3 minutes or until the eggs have set.

5 Add the prawns and crabmeat to the rice. Stir-fry for 1 minute. Season to taste with salt and pepper and add the sugar with the soy sauce. Stir to mix and spoon into a warmed serving dish. Garnish with a radish flower and sprinkle with freshly snipped and whole chives. Serve immediately.

cows' milk-free   egg-free   gluten-free   wheat-free   nut-free   vegetarian   vegan   seafood-free

Salmon Fish Cakes

Nutritional details

per 100 g

energy	154 kcals/647 kj
protein	12 g
carbohydrate	13 g
fat	6 g
fibre	1 g
sugar	2.3 g
sodium	0.2 g

Ingredients Serves 4

225 g/8 oz potatoes, peeled
450 g/1 lb salmon fillet, skinned
125 g/4 oz carrot,
    trimmed and peeled
2 tbsp grated lemon rind
2–3 tbsp freshly
    chopped coriander
1 medium egg yolk
salt and freshly ground
    black pepper
2 tbsp plain white flour
few fine sprays of oil

To serve:
prepared tomato sauce
tossed green salad
crusty bread

Step-by-step guide

1 Cube the potatoes and cook in lightly salted boiling water for 15 minutes. Drain and mash the potatoes. Place in a mixing bowl and reserve.

2 Place the salmon in a food processor and blend to form a chunky purée. Add the purée to the potatoes and mix together.

3 Coarsely grate the carrot and add to the fish with the lemon rind and the coriander.

4 Add the egg yolk, season to taste with salt and pepper, then gently mix the ingredients together. With damp hands form the mixture into four large fish cakes.

5 Coat in the flour and place on a plate. Cover loosely and chill for at least 30 minutes.

6 When ready to cook, spray a griddle pan with a few fine sprays of oil and heat the pan. When hot, add the fish cakes and cook on both sides for 3–4 minutes or until the fish is cooked. Add an extra spray of oil if needed during the cooking.

7 When the fish cakes are cooked, serve immediately with the tomato sauce, green salad and crusty bread.

cows' milk-free   egg-free   gluten-free   wheat-free   nut-free   vegetarian   vegan   seafood-free

Salmon Teriyaki with Noodles & Crispy Greens

Nutritional details

per 100 g

energy	196 kcals/813 kj
protein	12 g
carbohydrate	6 g
fat	14 g
fibre	0.9 g
sugar	1.5 g
sodium	0.5 g

Ingredients   Serves 4

350 g/12 oz salmon fillet
3 tbsp Japanese soy sauce
3 tbsp mirin or sweet sherry
3 tbsp sake
1 tbsp freshly grated root ginger
225 g/8 oz spring greens
vegetable oil for deep-frying
pinch of salt
½ tsp caster sugar
125 g/4 oz flat rice noodles

To garnish:
1 tbsp freshly chopped dill
sprigs of fresh dill
zest of ½ lemon

Step-by-step guide

1. Cut the salmon into paper-thin slices and place in a shallow dish.

Mix together the soy sauce, mirin or sherry, sake and the ginger. Pour over the salmon, cover and leave to marinate for 15–30 minutes.

2. Remove and discard the thick stalks from the spring greens. Lay several leaves on top of each other, roll up tightly, then shred finely.

3. Pour in enough oil to cover about 5 cm/2 inches of the wok. Deep-fry the greens in batches for about 1 minute each until crisp. Remove and drain on absorbent kitchen paper. Transfer to a serving dish, sprinkle with salt and sugar and toss together.

4. Place the noodles in a bowl and pour over warm water to cover. Leave to soak for 15–20 minutes until soft, then drain. With scissors cut into 15 cm/6 inch lengths.

5. Preheat the grill. Remove the salmon slices from the marinade, reserving the marinade for later, and arrange them in a single layer on a baking sheet. Grill for about 2 minutes, until lightly cooked, without turning.

6. When the oil in the wok is cool enough, tip most of it away, leaving about 1 tablespoon behind. Heat until hot, then add the noodles and the reserved marinade and stir-fry for 3–4 minutes. Tip the noodles into a large, warmed serving bowl and arrange the salmon slices on top, garnished with chopped dill, sprigs of fresh dill and lemon zest. Scatter with a little of the crispy greens and serve the rest separately.

✓ cows' milk-free ✓ egg-free ✓ gluten-free ✓ wheat-free ✓ nut-free ✓ vegetarian ✓ vegan ✓ seafood-free

Shredded Beef in Hoisin Sauce

Nutritional details

per 100 g

energy	151 kcals/633 kj
protein	14 g
carbohydrate	10 g
fat	6 g
fibre	0.6 g
sugar	1 g
sodium	0.3 g

Ingredients   Serves 4

2 celery sticks
125 g/4 oz carrots
450 g/1 lb rump steak
2 tbsp cornflour
salt and freshly ground
    black pepper
2 tbsp sunflower oil
4 spring onions, trimmed
    and chopped
2 tbsp light soy sauce
1 tbsp hoisin sauce
1 tbsp sweet chilli sauce
2 tbsp dry sherry
250 g pack fine egg thread noodles
1 tbsp freshly chopped
coriander

Step-by-step guide

1   Trim the celery and peel
the carrots, then cut into
fine matchsticks and reserve.

2   Place the steak between two sheets
of greaseproof paper or baking
parchment. Beat the steak with a
meat mallet or rolling pin until very
thin, then slice into strips. Season
the cornflour with salt and pepper
and use to coat the steak. Reserve.

3   Heat a wok, add the oil and when
hot, add the spring onions and cook
for 1 minute, then add the steak and
stir-fry for a further 3–4 minutes, or
until the meat is sealed.

4   Add the celery and carrot
matchsticks to the wok and stir-fry

for a further 2 minutes before
adding the soy, hoisin and chilli
sauces and the sherry. Bring to the
boil and simmer for 2–3 minutes,
or until the steak is tender and the
vegetables are cooked.

5   Plunge the fine egg noodles
into boiling water and leave for
4 minutes. Drain, then spoon
onto a large serving dish. Top with
the cooked shredded steak, then
sprinkle with chopped coriander
and serve immediately.

✓ cows' milk-free   ✓ egg-free   ✓ gluten-free   ✓ wheat-free   ✓ nut-free   ✓ vegetarian   ✓ vegan   ✓ seafood-free

Smoked Salmon Sushi

Nutritional details

per 100 g

energy	91 kcals/383 kj
protein	5 g
carbohydrate	15 g
fat	0.8 g
fibre	trace
sugar	4.7 g
sodium	0.9 g

Ingredients   Serves 4

175 g/6 oz sushi rice
2 tbsp rice vinegar
4 tsp caster sugar
½ tsp salt
2 sheets sushi nori
60 g/2½ oz smoked salmon
¼ cucumber, cut into fine strips

To serve:
wasabi
soy sauce
pickled ginger

Step-by-step guide

1 Rinse the rice thoroughly in cold water, until the water runs clear, then place in a pan with 300 ml/½ pint of water. Bring to the boil and cover with a tight-fitting lid. Reduce to a simmer and cook gently for 10 minutes. Turn the heat off, but keep the pan covered, to allow the rice to steam for a further 10 minutes.

2 In a small saucepan gently heat the rice vinegar, sugar and salt until the sugar has dissolved. When the rice has finished steaming, pour over the vinegar mixture and stir well. Empty the rice out on to a large flat surface – a chopping board or large plate is ideal. Fan the rice to cool and to produce a shinier finish.

3 Lay one sheet of sushi nori on a sushi mat. If you do not have a sushi mat, improvise with a stiff piece of fabric that is a little larger than the sushi nori. Spread with half the cooled rice. Dampen your hands while doing this – it helps to prevent the rice from sticking to your hands. On the nearest edge, place half the salmon and half the cucumber strips.

4 Roll up the rice and smoked salmon into a tight Swiss roll-like shape. Dampen the blade of a sharp knife and cut the sushi into slices about 2 cm/¾ inch thick. Repeat with the remaining sushi nori, rice, smoked salmon and cucumber. Serve with wasabi, soy sauce and pickled ginger.

cows' milk-free   egg-free   gluten-free   wheat-free   nut-free   vegetarian   vegan   seafood-free

Smoked Turkey Tagliatelle

Nutritional details

per 100 g

energy	79 kcals/334 kj
protein	8 g
carbohydrate	7 g
fat	2 g
fibre	0.5 g
sugar	1.4 g
sodium	0.3 g

Ingredients   Serves 4

2 tsp olive oil
1 bunch spring onions,
    trimmed and diagonally sliced
1 garlic clove,
    peeled and crushed
1 small courgette, trimmed,
    sliced and cut in half
4 tbsp dry white wine
400 g can chopped tomatoes
2 tbsp freshly shredded basil
salt and freshly ground
    black pepper
225 g/8 oz spinach and
    egg tagliatelle
225 g/8 oz smoked turkey breast,
    cut into strips
small fresh basil leaves,
    to garnish

Step-by-step guide

1 Heat the oil in a saucepan.
   Add the spring onions and garlic
   and gently cook for 2–3 minutes,
   until beginning to soften. Stir in
   the sliced courgette and cook
   for 1 minute.

2 Add the wine and let it bubble for
   1–2 minutes. Stir in the chopped
   tomatoes, bring to the boil and
   simmer uncovered over a low heat
   for 15 minutes, or until the
   courgettes are tender and the sauce
   slightly reduced. Stir the shredded
   basil into the sauce and season to
   taste with salt and pepper.

3 Meanwhile, bring a large pan
   of salted water to the boil.
   Add the tagliatelle and cook
   for 10 minutes, until 'al dente'
   or according to the packet
   instructions. Drain thoroughly.

4 Return the tagliatelle to the pan,
   add half the tomato sauce and
   toss together to coat the pasta
   thoroughly in the sauce. Cover
   with a lid and reserve.

5 Add the strips of turkey to the
   remaining sauce and heat gently
   for 2–3 minutes until piping hot.

6 Divide the tagliatelle among four
   serving plates. Spoon over the
   sauce, garnish with basil leaves
   and serve immediately.

✔ cows' milk-free   ✔ egg-free   ✔ gluten-free   ✔ wheat-free   ✔ nut-free   ✔ vegetarian   ✔ vegan   ✔ seafood-free

Sweet-&-Sour Prawns with Noodles

Nutritional details

per 100 g

energy	73 kcals/307 kj
protein	5 g
carbohydrate	11 g
fat	1 g
fibre	0.5 g
sugar	7 g
sodium	0.4 g

Ingredients   Serves 4

425 g can pineapple pieces
   in natural juice
1 green pepper, deseeded
   and cut into quarters
1 tbsp sunflower oil
1 onion, cut into thin wedges
3 tbsp soft brown sugar
150 ml/¼ pint chicken stock
4 tbsp wine vinegar
1 tbsp tomato purée
1 tbsp light soy sauce
1 tbsp cornflour
350 g/12 oz raw tiger
   prawns, peeled
225 g/8 oz pak choi,
   shredded
350 g/12 oz medium
   egg noodles
coriander leaves,
   to garnish

Step-by-step guide

1   Make the sauce by draining the pineapple and reserving 2 tablespoons of the juice.

2   Remove the membrane from the quartered peppers and cut into thin strips.

3   Heat the oil in a saucepan. Add the onion and pepper and cook for about 4 minutes or until the onion has softened.

4   Add the pineapple, sugar, stock, vinegar, tomato purée and soy sauce.

5   Bring the sauce to the boil and simmer for about 4 minutes. Blend the cornflour with the reserved pineapple juice and stir into the pan, stirring until thickened.

6   Clean the prawns if needed. Wash the pak choi thoroughly, then shred.

7   Add the prawns and pak choi to the sauce. Simmer gently for 3 minutes or until the prawns are cooked and have turned pink.

8   Cook the noodles in boiling water for 4–5 minutes until just tender.

9   Drain and arrange the noodles on a warmed plate and pour over the sweet-and-sour prawns. Garnish with coriander leaves and serve immediately.

cows' milk-free   egg-free   gluten-free   wheat-free   nut-free   vegetarian   vegan   seafood-free

43

Sweet-&-Sour Rice with Chicken

Nutritional details

per 100 g

energy	126 kcals/528 kj
protein	14 g
carbohydrate	12 g
fat	3 g
fibre	0.5 g
sugar	5.7 g
sodium	0.2 g

Ingredients   Serves 4

4 spring onions
2 tsp sesame oil
1 tsp Chinese five spice powder
450 g/1 lb chicken breast,
    cut into cubes
1 tbsp vegetable oil
1 garlic clove,
    peeled and crushed
1 medium onion, peeled and
    sliced into thin wedges
225 g/8 oz long-grain white rice
600 ml/1 pint water
4 tbsp tomato ketchup
1 tbsp tomato purée
2 tbsp honey
1 tbsp vinegar
1 tbsp dark soy sauce
1 carrot, peeled and
    cut into matchsticks

Step-by-step guide

1 Trim the spring onions, then cut lengthways into fine strips. Drop into a large bowl of iced water and reserve.

2 Mix together the sesame oil and Chinese five spice powder and use to rub into the cubed chicken. Heat the wok, then add the oil and when hot, cook the garlic and onion for 2–3 minutes, or until transparent and softened.

3 Add the chicken and stir-fry over a medium-high heat until the chicken is golden and cooked through.

Using a slotted spoon, remove from the wok and keep warm.

4 Stir the rice into the wok and add the water, tomato ketchup, tomato purée, honey, vinegar and soy sauce. Stir well to mix. Bring to the boil, then simmer until almost all of the liquid is absorbed. Stir in the carrot and reserved chicken and continue to cook for 3–4 minutes.

5 Drain the spring onions, which will have become curly. Garnish with the spring onion curls and serve immediately with the rice and chicken.

cows' milk-free   egg-free   gluten-free   wheat-free   nut-free   vegetarian   vegan   seafood-free

Teriyaki Beef

Nutritional details

per 100 g

energy	138 kcals/580 kj
protein	17 g
carbohydrate	8 g
fat	5 g
fibre	0.2 g
sugar	1.9 g
sodium	0.6 g

Ingredients   Serves 4

550 g/1¼ lb rump
    or sirloin steak
1 medium onion,
    peeled and finely sliced
5 cm/2 inch piece of fresh
    root ginger, peeled and
    coarsely chopped
1 bird's-eye chilli, deseeded
    and finely chopped
6 tbsp light soy sauce
2 tbsp sake or sweet sherry
1 tbsp lemon juice
1 tsp clear honey
250 g/9 oz glutinous rice
sunflower oil, for spraying

To garnish:
carrot matchsticks
daikon matchsticks
sprigs of fresh coriander

Step-by-step guide

1 Trim the steak, discarding any fat or gristle, and place in a non-metallic shallow dish. Scatter the sliced onion over the steak. Mix the ginger with the chilli and sprinkle over the steak and onion.

2 Blend the soy sauce with the sake or sherry, the lemon juice and honey. Stir well, then pour over the steak and onion. Cover and leave to marinate in the refrigerator for at least 1 hour, or longer if time permits. Turn the steak over, or occasionally spoon the marinade over the meat, during this time.

3 Place the rice in a saucepan with 450 ml/¾ pint of water and cook until tender. Drain if necessary, then pack into four warmed and oiled individual moulds. Quickly invert onto four individual warm plates and keep warm.

4 Spray or brush a griddle pan with oil, then heat until really hot. Drain the steak and cook in the griddle pan for 2–3 minutes on each side, or until cooked to personal preference. Remove from the pan and slice thinly. Arrange on the warm serving plates, garnish with the carrot and daikon matchsticks and coriander sprigs, then serve.

cows' milk-free   egg-free   gluten-free   wheat-free   nut-free   vegetarian   vegan   seafood-free

45

Thai Fish Cakes

Nutritional details

per 100 g

energy	85 kcals/361 kj
protein	18 g
carbohydrate	1 g
fat	1 g
fibre	0.2 g
sugar	0.2 g
sodium	0.6 g

Ingredients   Serves 4

1 red chilli, deseeded
    and roughly chopped
4 tbsp roughly chopped
    fresh coriander
1 garlic clove,
    peeled and crushed
2 spring onions, trimmed
    and roughly chopped
1 lemon grass, outer
    leaves discarded and
    roughly chopped
75 g/3 oz prawns,
    thawed if frozen
275 g/10 oz cod fillet,
    skinned, pin bones
    removed and cubed
salt and freshly ground
    black pepper
sweet chilli dipping sauce,
    to serve

Step-by-step guide

1   Preheat the oven to 190°C/
    375°F/Gas Mark 5. Place the chilli,
    coriander, garlic, spring onions
    and lemon grass in a food
    processor and blend together.

2   Pat the prawns and cod
    dry with kitchen paper.

3   Add to the food processor
    and blend until the mixture is
    roughly chopped.

4   Season to taste with salt and
    pepper and blend to mix.

5   Dampen your hands, then shape
    heaped tablespoons of the
    mixture into 12 little patties.

6   Place the patties on a lightly oiled
    baking sheet and cook in the
    preheated oven for 12–15 minutes
    or until piping hot and cooked
    through. Turn the patties over
    halfway through the cooking time.

7   Serve the fish cakes immediately
    with the sweet chilli sauce
    for dipping.

✓ cows' milk-free   ✓ egg-free   ✓ gluten-free   ✓ wheat-free   ✓ nut-free   ✓ vegetarian   ✓ vegan   ✓ seafood-free

Turkey Escalopes with Apricot Chutney

Nutritional details

per 100 g

energy	143 kcals/605 kj
protein	21 g
carbohydrate	11 g
fat	2 g
fibre	1.1 g
sugar	9.1 g
sodium	trace

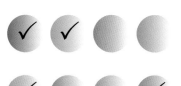

Ingredients   Serves 4

4 x 175–225 g/6–8 oz
    turkey steaks
1 tbsp plain flour
salt and freshly ground
    black pepper
1 tbsp olive oil
flat leaf parsley sprigs,
    to garnish
orange wedges, to serve

For the apricot chutney:

125 g/4 oz no-need-to-soak dried
    apricots, chopped
1 red onion, peeled and
    finely chopped
1 tsp grated fresh root ginger
2 tbsp caster sugar
finely grated rind of ½ orange
125 ml/4 fl oz fresh
    orange juice
125 ml/4 fl oz ruby port
1 whole clove

Step-by-step guide

1 Put a turkey steak on to a sheet of non-pvc clingfilm or non-stick baking parchment. Cover with a second sheet.

2 Using a rolling pin, gently pound the turkey until the meat is flattened to about 5 mm/¼ inch thick. Repeat to make four escalopes. Mix the flour with the salt and pepper and use to lightly dust the turkey escalopes.

3 Put the turkey escalopes on a board or baking tray and cover with a piece of non-pvc clingfilm or non-stick baking parchment. Chill in the refrigerator until ready to cook.

4 For the apricot chutney, put the apricots, onion, ginger, sugar, orange rind, orange juice, port and clove into a saucepan.

5 Slowly bring to the boil and simmer uncovered for 10 minutes, stirring occasionally, until thick and syrupy.

6 Remove the clove and stir in the chopped coriander.

7 Heat the oil in a pan and chargriddle the turkey escalopes, in two batches if necessary, for 3–4 minutes on each side until golden brown and tender.

8 Spoon the chutney on to four individual serving plates. Place a turkey escalope on top of each spoonful of chutney. Garnish with sprigs of parsley and serve immediately with orange wedges.

cows' milk-free   egg-free   gluten-free   wheat-free   nut-free   vegetarian   vegan   seafood-free

47

Warm Potato, Pear & Pecan Salad

Nutritional details

per 100 g

energy	112 kcals/472 kj
protein	2 g
carbohydrate	12 g
fat	7 g
fibre	1.6 g
sugar	3.1 g
sodium	trace

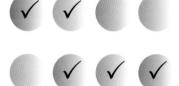

Ingredients   Serves 4

900 g/2 lb new potatoes, preferably
    red-skinned, unpeeled
salt and freshly ground black pepper
1 tsp Dijon mustard
2 tsp white wine vinegar
3 tbsp groundnut oil
1 tbsp hazelnut or walnut oil
2 tsp poppy seeds
2 firm ripe dessert pears
2 tsp lemon juice
175 g/6 oz baby spinach leaves
75 g/3 oz toasted pecan nuts

Step-by-step guide

1   Scrub the potatoes, then cook in a
    saucepan of lightly salted boiling
    water for 15 minutes, or until
    tender. Drain, cut into halves, or
    quarters if large, and place in a
    serving bowl.

2   In a small bowl or jug, whisk
    together the mustard and vinegar.
    Gradually add the oils until the
    mixture begins to thicken. Stir in
    the poppy seeds and season to
    taste with salt and pepper.

3   Pour about two thirds of the
    dressing over the hot potatoes
    and toss gently to coat. Leave
    until the potatoes have soaked up
    the dressing and are just warm.

4   Meanwhile, quarter and core the
    pears. Cut into thin slices, then
    sprinkle with the lemon juice to
    prevent them from going brown.
    Add to the potatoes with the
    spinach leaves and toasted pecan
    nuts. Gently mix together.

5   Drizzle the remaining dressing
    over the salad. Serve immediately
    before the spinach starts to wilt.

✓ cows' milk-free   ✓ egg-free   ✓ gluten-free   ✓ wheat-free   ✓ nut-free   ✓ vegetarian   ✓ vegan   ✓ seafood-free